GETTING THE CHEMISTRY RIGHT

How a start-up developed a global market leading product and secured a multi-million Euro buyout

DAVID HORAN

Copyright © 2021 David Horan
All rights reserved. This book or any portion thereof
may not be reproduced or used in any manner whatsoever
without the express written permission of the author
except for the use of brief quotations in a book review.

Printed in Ireland and the UK

www.printmybook.com

First Printing, 2021
ISBN 9798724143219

This book is dedicated to my parents, Martin and Nancy, for all their hard work, vision and generosity, and to my wife Sue for her constant support and encouragement.

All proceeds from the sale of this book will be donated to Marymount Hospice Cork.

Contents

Foreword	1
Introduction	3
Chapter 1 – Thinking Inside the Box	6
Chapter 2 – Developing a Strategy	27
Chapter 3 – Selling Solutions	50
Chapter 4 – An Offer and a New Deal	74
Chapter 5 – Take Off	100
Chapter 6 – Looking East	119
Chapter 7 –The Product Loss Breakthrough	135
Chapter 8 – The Struggle to Stay Independent	156
Chapter 9 – Stress	177
Chapter 10 – Acquisition	196
Chapter 11 – Aftermath	220
Acknowledgements	235

Foreword by Simon Coveney TD, Minister for Foreign Affairs

Martin and Nancy Horan have been friends of mine for more than twenty years. They are community people; as interested in changing the local parish as changing the world through politics or technology. Family comes before everything else. They're generous, thoughtful, successful but always modest; the kind of people you want to spend time with.

I never thought this book would be written. Focusing on past success is not something the Horan family do publicly. Instead, they focus on the future. It's what makes them so interesting: the next innovation, the new opportunity. David Horan is understated but driven like his parents. This book shares the compelling journey of a small family business that would become a global market leader. In less than five years, the value of BioTector would take off, from €2.6m to almost €45m.

Some stories are more than worth telling, this one is certainly worth reading. It's told with such honesty and authenticity that it stands out from the many other SME business development books.

Anyone trying to build a business, manage family

relations, deal with stress, motivate a team to design a game-changing product, develop global markets, work with multinationals and ultimately realise value through acquisition, will find so many lessons in this book.

There's a reason why the biblical story of David and Goliath endures. We all want to believe that success is possible, even in the face of impossible odds. Being small, being the underdog, is no barrier. It's what motivates entrepreneurship. In fact, this story is proof that to be underestimated by giants can be turned to advantage.

Honesty, team excellence, continuous improvement and a singular focus on building the best product of its type has driven BioTector to extraordinary success.

This team that Martin, Nancy and David built with partners across the globe would command respect and ultimately a value that resulted in a stunning acquisition story.

You don't have to be in business to relate to this book. We can all take from David's personal account: the ambition, the doubts, the risks, the successes, the strain, the excitement.

There are so many life lessons and no small amount of inspiration in this book, as we relate it to our own search for recognition, achievement and contentment. It's a great read.

Introduction

Looking back at the succession of obstacles that my parents faced when they first started BioTector, you kind of have to wonder at why they took it on in the first place. We had a flawed technology and a market that resented buying it, while our competition was way better resourced than we were. And yet between us, we managed to build a product that would go on to become a market leader globally, and would be sold into fifty-two countries around the world. BioTector continues to be a wonderful Irish success story, but you'd have to say that that success looked highly improbable back in 1995 when Mom and Dad first set up the company.

There are many reasons why we achieved what we achieved, but the common thread that runs though this story is the drive to stay in control of our own destiny. We never went with the flow, we were constantly stopping and standing up to check where we were, to make sure we were heading exactly where we wanted to go. That's not an easy thing to do when you're a small company going up against big companies. But we had tremendous faith in our people, and that gave us the confidence to take the risks we needed to take. This was a family business, and family businesses can often falter in the move between one generation and the next. Myself and Mom and Dad managed to work particularly well together – each of us had a different skill set; Mom was great on the financials, Dad was the ideas man and I concentrated on growth. All of these skills were critical in getting us to where we got.

Four years on from leaving the company, I felt compelled to get our story down in print. For one thing, it's simply a great story, of success against the odds. Also, I'm sometimes asked to share it with companies who have similar growth ambitions. There are so many different elements to our story, so many interdependent dynamics that it was hard to disentangle one thing from another. I needed to get it all straight in my own head before I could use it to help anyone else. Writing it down has been really helpful from that point of view.

I've read a lot of business books, a lot of 'how-to' books, but I've often found them hard to relate to. No matter how logical, I find it difficult to apply the instruction to the real world. Not everything in the BioTector story is going to resonate with everyone, but I'm hoping that there will be something here for everyone, something that those facing similar challenges may be able to take away and use. There's been no attempt to airbrush anything, or pretend that it was one success after another. This is warts and all. We made tons of mistakes, and they're all here. The hope is that by seeing where we went wrong, you can avoid making the same errors, and that by seeing what worked for us, you can capitalise on that.

It was a wonderful experience, but it wasn't an easy ride.

Today, myself, Mom and Dad continue to work together. We invest in companies with great potential, and which we feel we could work well with. I talk about this in more detail in the last chapter. If you have a company and you think that we might be able to help you realise your growth ambitions, do please get in touch.

David Horan, March 2021

davidhoran@raffeenpark.com

Chapter 1 – Thinking Inside the Box

When you write about a story like ours, the path we followed can seem obvious, but the truth is that none of it was obvious. There were multiple points where anything could have happened, where we could have collapsed, or pulled the plug or taken a wrong turn and ended up failing badly. It took around fifteen years to figure out how to get where we eventually got. And the deck was stacked against us. Most of our competitors were huge, multinational, household name corporations. They owned the market. There were all sorts of barriers to entry. We were a small, Irish based family business that employed a handful of people. On paper, we shouldn't have succeeded. On paper, we were no threat.

But we had an amazing group of people. Really, I feel that we could have done anything together. And that can be a pitfall. With the spread of abilities in the company, the temptation was to do everything. It took a lot of discipline – especially when we began to make money – to remain focused on one thing and to commit ourselves to being brilliant at that, to restrict our innovation to a tight circle of applications. This is thinking *inside* the box. Understanding customer needs and only delivering on those that don't drag us out of a tight, focused space. So there was a lot of saying "No. Let's focus on this, and this only."

Most people in business know about the hedgehog concept, the idea that your greatest opportunity lies at the intersection of three things; your passion, your economic engine and the thing that you can be best at. That's what happened with BioTector. We were supremely passionate about something, and in time, we became best in the world at it. The third part of the equation – making money out of it – that came more slowly. But it would be wrong to think that we took the hedgehog concept and set out to apply it to our business. It was really only as we began to succeed that we realised that what we were doing corresponded closely with the model.

Irish Superior Safety Systems

My parents, Martin and Nancy Horan spent five years in Canada when they were first married. They had always wanted to run their own business, but on their return home, Dad started working for Chubb. Chubb was and remains one of the biggest names in the UK and Ireland in safety systems – fire alarms, smoke alarms and so on. It was while working for them that he realised that customer service tended to be quite poor in this sector, and that Cork based companies had to rely on Dublin based service providers.

He had spotted a gap in the market, and together, he and Mom set up Irish Superior Safety Systems (ISSS) to supply fire and gas alarm systems. The company became so successful that in time, they found themselves competing with Chubb for much bigger customers, including a range of international pharmaceutical companies in Ringaskiddy, Co. Cork. Irish Superior actually became bigger than Chubb in Ireland – employing over fifty people at its peak. In the end, Chubb would buy them out.

Dad always maintained that the success of ISSS as a family enterprise owes a great deal to the division of labour between Mom and himself. Dad looked after the sales and the technical side of the business while mom looked after the secretarial and most importantly the invoicing, debt collection and financial control. This partnership helped avoid the busy fool syndrome that's often the downfall of start-ups. Cash flow was never an issue.

The story of their first company is fascinating in its own right, but I'm not going to go into it here. Instead,

I'll stick with how Dad's experience with Irish Superior Safety Systems lead to BioTector.

My parents' company sold and maintained a wide variety of safety equipment. When you're a distributor, you're always looking out for new systems to supply to existing customers. You're always asking yourself, how can I add to my portfolio? It's perhaps the easiest way to grow the business. So instead of just fire alarms and smoke detectors, could you add gas detection? Suppression systems maybe?

In the early nineties, Cork became one of the first local authorities to insist that local industry in general and the pharmaceutical industry in particular monitor their emissions. This is a highly technical area, but one in which ISSS already had some expertise, which is why Dad decided to zero in on it. New products necessitate training, so Dad and his team underwent extensive training in a range of analytical technologies.

TOC

One of the systems he became intimately acquainted with at the time was an online TOC analyser. TOC stands for Total Organic Carbon. This is one of the most important metrics for assessing the organic pollution in waste water. There are two types of TOC analyser, online and laboratory. Lab analysers, as the name suggests, measure the organic carbon present in a lab sample, while an online analyser continually assesses the carbon content in a live setting.

The problem was that the online analyser that Dad maintained was extremely unreliable, to put it delicately. No sooner had one problem been sorted out than he'd get a call. "It's broken again. Come in and fix it." And he'd hardly be home again before he'd get another call. "It's broken again. Come in and fix it."

Despite the shortcomings of the system, the result it provided was absolutely crucial to the customer. At the time, if a factory had a TOC analyser, it sat right at the end of the pipe, after waste water treatment, just before discharge into the water course. Making sure the water was clean before it was released was absolutely crucial. This is why the measurement was vital. Legislation wasn't as tight as it is now in this area, but the cluster of pharmaceuticals that Dad was dealing with knew what was coming down the line, plus of course, they needed to protect their reputation locally. Nobody wanted to pollute the river or the sea.

The Search for a Better Technology

At the time, every single manufacturer of online TOC analysers across the world was using one of two technologies. UV Persulfate or high temperature thermal. Both could deliver an accurate result, but both had huge maintenance issues. If either took in clean water only, they'd work fine. But you're monitoring on an exceptions basis. You want to know when something goes wrong, when something comes through the pipe that shouldn't come through the pipe. It was at this point – when contaminants flowed into the system – that both became clogged up and struggled to measure anything.

In the course of his work, Dad came across a Norwegian project that was trialling an entirely new TOC analysis process which involved sodium hydroxide and ozone. On the face of it, it seemed to solve the reliability issue. The system did not get quite as clogged up when anything other than clean water passed through it. But while it was more robust, the downside was that the measurement wasn't as accurate as either of the two existing methods. BioTector was the name of the product.

Dad explored the technology thoroughly and decided that while the accuracy deficit was a significant issue, with sufficient research and effort, it might well be possible to fix it. Tor was the other factor in the equation. Tor Anders was a big, exuberant, larger than life character, who had been involved in the development of the new technology from the beginning. He had already secured a number of sales in Europe – including to Dow Chemicals in Germany – and believed that he could secure many more.

Mom and Dad bought out the technology and set up Pollution Control Systems in Cork in 1995. Tor Anders had a fixed shareholding with an option to increase this if he met projected targets. He began flying around the world, making sales into industries – like pulp and paper – which were particularly 'dirty', too dirty for either of the two traditional technologies to work. Despite his efforts, sales did not really take off. We weren't covering our costs or anything like it. While Tor had managed to establish distributors in a range of diverse locations (Taiwan, Texas and Japan to name three) each sale took a lot of work and Tor's optimistic projections never really materialised. Though it was a separate entity, Pollution Control Systems relied heavily on support from ISSS, and for this reason, it could limp along at a loss. We were effectively an R&D company, and would remain so for some years.

It was the fact that there were sales that continued

to give Dad hope. There were those out there who were willing to invest in the system despite its short-comings.

Seamus O'Mahony

During those early years, there was one other guy who was central to the BioTector story. Seamus O'Mahony had worked with Dad in Irish Superior for years, and when Dad started Pollution Control Systems, he invited Seamus back to become head of operations and R&D. Seamus was a qualified electrician and had extensive experience both in the service sector and with analytical equipment. In addition, he had also completed a degree in electronics and embedded system design. Seamus would go on to be awarded degree qualifications in organic chemistry, physics and business.

He has an incredible brain, with the greatest eye for detail that I've ever seen. He could turn his hand to almost anything. Seamus was capable of getting down among the electrons and understanding processes at a sub-atomic level. All you had to do was point Seamus at a problem, ask him to figure it out, and he would drive relentlessly towards the solution.

While Dad was always happy to get his hands dirty, he was still the ideas man, always very positive, full of belief in the potential of the project. Seamus was the opposite. He would say, "It probably won't work. I'm going to test it, and we'll see." It was the collision of those dynamics, of the visionary and the details man that drove the creativity and ultimately the success of the company.

Seamus has an astonishing memory. We used to number each analyser – open the door and you'd see it on the inside. No.43 – if it was the forty third one we'd made. Up until we built about the 160th unit, Seamus would be able to tell you exactly where each of the analysers was installed. Give him the number and he'd tell you what company, what country, when it went in and its precise configuration. When he came on board, Mom and Dad gave him a minority shareholding in BioTector.

It's also important to point out just how important Mom was in the BioTector story. She doesn't take a central role in all that follows, but without her, there's no doubt that we would never have succeeded. Dad was free to pursue his goal only because she was there to take care of all of the boring stuff – company formation, invoices, payroll, VAT returns, rental agreements…the list goes on. I've seen a lot of companies begun by engineers or inventors only to fall flat because they lacked the skills to get money in. If Mom hadn't been there to make sure that everyone got paid, there's no doubt but that we would have floundered as well.

New Directions

To give you some idea of what the analyser looks like, BioTector is a reinforced box about five feet tall, equipped with pumps, valves, reactors and chambers. It's effectively a small factory in itself – filled with moving parts, all sourced from a variety of different suppliers. A CO_2 analyser from one place, a pump from another, a section of tubing from another and so on. In the early years, Dad used his various contacts from his ISSS days to trial the analyser in live conditions. These included a range of pharmaceutical companies in Cork, as well as a number of local authorities. This facilitated a series of improvements to the technology. Within a couple of years however, Dad realised that he now had a choice. Option one was to take what they had and push it as hard as they could. That's what Tor wanted to do. "Let's just fly to more countries, and find more applications." But Dad's instinct was that the system simply wasn't good enough yet.

The ambition that began to take shape in his mind was this: Double down on the research and set out to create the best analyser in the world. This was what excited him.

This was where his passion lay. The point is that there was a pressing need, not just in industry, but in the wider world. If we had an analyser that could run maintenance-free and accurately detect pollutants before they hit the river, everyone would benefit. It was this idea that caught his imagination and fired everything that happened next.

O'Kelly Sutton is a strategic consultancy that features regularly in the BioTector story. Every so often, Dad or I would say, "Right, this is just too big a decision to take without outside advice, let's bring in someone to get a clear, dispassionate view." Other times, we would simply call up Paul O'Kelly and bounce ideas off him. "We're thinking of doing this. What do you think?"

Paul and Dad sat down and went through the options. Paul asked Dad how much Tor was costing the company. Between his salary and the constant flying to and fro, this was a substantial sum.

"If you used that money to improve the analyser," he asked, "would that make it easier to market your product?"

The answer to this was an unambiguous 'yes'. Instead of pushing a flawed product, he would focus on R&D and drive towards that compelling idea.

The best TOC analyser in the world.

So Dad bought Tor out and they parted ways amicably.

So began a deep-dive into the product. What we found was that nearly all of the components in the analyser were suboptimal. All had been designed for other applications and so had to be adapted – often extensively – to work in the analyser. Dad and Seamus realised that the only way they would make a success of the system and solve the accuracy problem was to customise each component in-house.

So now, Seamus began redesigning everything with the worst, the dirtiest, the most polluting customer situation in mind. Suppose it's a refinery and the wastewater suddenly has pure oil in it. What's going to happen to this pump and that valve? What will happen to the tubing? Or suppose it's the dairy industry, and you've got full-fat milk coming down, or yogurt. What's that going to do to the analyser?

It helped that both Dad and Seamus had such strong service backgrounds. They may have had different perspectives on business challenges but when it came to service, they were of one mind. Both constantly asked "What's the weak point in this component? Where's that going to get clogged? How long is that going to live? What happens if you get grease in here?"

They rebuilt the analyser with the maintenance person in mind. Components were placed so that they were easy to get at, easy to open, easy to replace.

Developing the Perfect Product

With Tor gone, the revenue stream was effectively turned off, so to keep it ticking over, Dad took on the sales role. This involved extensive travel. He focused on industries where TOC analysis was already in place, where the limitations of existing technologies were well understood. Corporations in these sectors invariably had a programme of continuous replacement and upgrading of existing analysers. Our goal was to present BioTector as a viable alternative, as the product that could end this endless cycle of repair, upgrade and replacement. One of the consequences of this focus was that our sales presentations were highly technical. More about that later.

Now, in addition to leading the R&D effort in the office, Dad was visiting customers and making the odd sale here and there. Thanks to Irish Superior, he didn't need to take a salary. This was of course a luxury that few start ups can afford, and nor was it a situation that could continue indefinitely. All of these trips out to clients around the world served a dual purpose. Dad was talking to customers, trying to understand their problems, and of course, observing closely how the analyser was working in real situations.

The local pharma companies were really great in helping us out at this point. Dad or Seamus would say to the customer, "Look, we think this pump might be better. Do you mind if we come over and pop it into the analyser?" And they would invariably say, "As long as you keep it running and there are no side effects, go ahead." So in addition to the R&D work in the factory, we were able to keep three or four reference sites under constant supervision.

We were always testing things. Always. You'd walk into the factory and see a bank of pumps running, with a variety of different tubes hanging out of them. If anyone suggested changing any component, it was always, well, how many hours testing have you run up? Nothing was released to the client until it was tested, tested, tested.

These tests were gruelling. The team basically set out to try to wreck each new component. Suppose a pump was supposed to pulse once every ten minutes in the analyser. In a test environment, we'd set it up to go non-stop for twenty-four hours. In a few weeks, you would have racked up the pump's entire onsite lifetime, so you could see whether or not it wore out. Does any part degrade? If it does, then move on. Find, or build a better one. If not, then you have a viable component. And once you're satisfied that it survives ok on its own, it's time to test it within the analyser. Does it work properly with all other components? Are there unintended consequences?

The goal, from a maintenance point of view, was that we would build something that you would not have to look at for six months. The analyser would be like a car. You could put the worst kind of sludge through it and it would clean itself up without anyone having to come near it. Then, once every six months, you give it a four-hour service and it runs perfectly for another six months. By contrast, our competitors would all have components that needed to be checked every three or four days. We were aiming for a standard that would put us so far ahead of the competition that we would be untouchable.

For the record, the problems with those two traditional TOC testing methodologies continue today. Others have tried to find a fourth technology and a fifth technology, but they never got there. One of our biggest competitors – one of the biggest companies in the world in fact – threw millions at the problem and never cracked it.

Curiosity

Dad and Seamus loved the process of discovery. They loved pulling things apart. "That broke? Wonderful! Let's go figure out why." No failure was ever seen as bad because there was something to be learned from it. If there was one word to summarise the culture that began to emerge in the fledgling company, it was 'curiosity'. How did that work? Why did that happen?

All of the guys in R&D, including Dad and Seamus, had pet projects. We had our main focus and our targets and timelines, but there was always enough flexibility for people to run with ideas. It became a problem sometimes, because you've so many pet projects and you're trying to get things done, but despite this, we always encouraged that flexibility. It motivated people and encouraged innovation. Without that, we wouldn't have been able to drive the continuous improvements that were absolutely vital to the success of the business.

It was a necessary retention tool as well. We were operating in a niche, trying to do one thing better than anyone else. To do that we needed highly creative problem solvers. Allowing them the latitude to run with an idea gave them the playtime they needed to stay motivated, to stay engaged with core issues. As a result, we never had a problem finding and holding onto great people.

We had a big canteen in the factory where Dad encouraged mixing and mingling. It might have looked like they were wasting time, but he had discovered in Irish Superior that getting people together to discuss things and share information was hugely beneficial to the company.

Don and Mack

In the course of Dad's travels, he signed two customers that would turn out to be really important in the BioTector story. Mack Keeter of Dow Chemicals and Don Lanoux of BASF. Both were based in the US, both – like Dad – had service backgrounds, and both had worked their way up to positions of significant influence in their respective companies. Several of the courses I went on when I joined the company talked about the importance of finding 'inside influencers' in target companies – people who can become advocates for your business within theirs. That's what Mack and Don were. They had considerable influence over which analyser would go into their factories around the world. And like Dad and Seamus, they knew just how bad the legacy technologies were, and were always really passionate about trying to solve the analyser problem. Crucially, they saw the potential in BioTector early and became enthusiastic advocates. They saw that the world was changing, and that as regulations tightened and reputation became more important, reliable online TOC analysis would become more critical. Lab analysis delivered results late, too late to be useful. Online analysis delivered results on the fly, and that's what would be needed in the years ahead. A better online analyser was vital because the measurement it provided would be sought by a wide range of industries around the world. Their perspective and support gave Dad great confidence. This could be really big.

Accuracy

So while we were making headway with the maintenance issue, the accuracy problem remained, and it was this, more than anything else, that was stifling the growth of the company. Our accuracy varied between plus or minus 10% and plus or minus 15% when the other two technologies were getting a 3% margin of error. Dad knew that if we didn't improve our numbers, it wouldn't matter how maintenance-free the analyser might be, we would never succeed. So we set up a project which we simply called *Get The Accuracy Right*.

The problem was a flaw in the chemistry. I don't want to get too technical about it but basically the oxidation process in the analyser's reactor breaks the incoming liquid down into its component parts – nitrogen, phosphorous, carbon and so on. The more carbon, the more pollution. The problem was that the chemical reaction wasn't releasing all of the carbon and we could not figure out why.

We put huge amounts of time and energy into this, but got nowhere.

Seamus was leading these efforts, but it was while he was doing something else entirely that the breakthrough came. There was a slight problem with clogging in a pump and he was trialling a new inline filter to protect it. He installed the pump with its new filter in a test analyser and went home for the evening. The following day, the analyser's carbon reading was a little higher than he would have expected. Most people would have shrugged this off, since it wasn't relevant to the test he was running, but Seamus isn't like most people. This slightly-higher-than-expected reading piqued his interest. He was curious. The only thing that was different was the filter, so he took it out and examined it. He noticed straightaway that the silver coating on the inside had degraded slightly, had worn away. This begged the following question: Had a little bit of silver gotten into the chemical reaction and changed things somehow?

The Eureka Moment

According to company legend, all of this happened on St. Valentine's Day. Seamus went down to the local jewellers and bought a silver chain – not for his wife, but for his analyser. He brought it back and literally popped it into the reactor. The following day, the result was up again. What appeared to be happening was that the silver was catalysing the reaction, releasing the last few atoms of carbon that the process up to that point had been unable to reach. Straight away, our accuracy shot up. In one fell swoop we were right up there with our competitors.

The problem? Silver is expensive. So Seamus began trawling through the periodic table, looking for something that had the properties of silver but was a little cheaper. It didn't take him too long to discover that manganese would do the job just as well. And that was it. Problem solved.

Dad's instinct, as soon as we made that breakthrough, was to patent it – this despite the fact that we were still a long way from making any real money on the analyser. Patenting is an expensive process, and isn't always worthwhile. At the time, royalties on patents were tax free. That was a key incentive. Of course by the time we began making money from it, the incentive had been scrapped. In any case, Seamus did the necessary paperwork and we were eventually granted a patent that proved to be very durable. Several years later, the chemistry that facilitated our success came under a lot of scrutiny. One Texas-based company spent a considerable sum trying to break it, but ultimately failed because of that patent.

Dad also got some great advice at this point. He created a separate company and placed the ownership of the patent there. This gave us the option of parcelling out the value of the company in a different way if the need ever arose.

Throughout this phase, our strategy was very clear. Build the best analyser in the world. We now knew that in essence, we had done that. There would be further improvements and refinements, but BioTector was now as accurate as any other product in the marketplace, and so much more robust.

So we had our great product. The next task was to build the great company that could deliver on its potential.

Chapter 2 – Developing a Strategy

Up until now, because our focus had remained almost exclusively on the technology, we'd had very little organic growth. Of the fifteen people in the company, nine were working in R&D.

One of the guys, Ali Demir was Turkish and had a doctorate in chemistry. Over time, he became absolutely crucial. So did Ian O'Mahoney. He began building analyser prototypes and would end up as our production manager, and did vital work in developing our policies and processes. Dave Ruzicka from the Czech Republic was one of our earliest hires. As the main software engineer, he brought a new discipline and expertise to the company and would go on to play a central role in many of our innovations and developments. Piotr Braatz and Marek Pawlukowiec, both Polish, were central figures on the R&D team. Jayne Powis, who's English, worked in sales and admin, but that doesn't capture how important she was to the company, in sales, in processing, in HR, in everything.

While we had no written policies or anything like that, we did have unwritten core values that everyone implicitly subscribed to. The drive to create the best analyser drove the commitment to become product leaders. Alongside that, we committed to looking after the customer, ensuring that the product would be easy to maintain and specifically that it wouldn't need maintenance more often than every six months. Everybody bought into these ideas. As we grew, we began to put it down on paper, but at the beginning, it was simply a lived culture that grew up around Dad and Seamus.

Barriers to Entry

One of the big issues in the sector we found ourselves in is that there were substantial barriers to entry. Redesigning the analyser, creating each individual component and testing them to the limit – this was an expensive business, which, at €40,000, made our analyser very expensive. In many cases, we were no less than twice the price of the competition. It was a great product, but it was also a super expensive product. This was a big issue. Our two great advocates, Mack Keeter in Dow and Don Lanoux in BASF were always telling us that if they were to recommend specifying BioTector across their organisations, they would have a lot of explaining to do.

It wasn't just price. Ours was also a non-standard process. Industrial technology is regulated by what are called DIN norms. German in origin, these are agreed international process standardisations which are reviewed every five years. As far as DIN norms were concerned, the only acceptable means of TOC analysis were the two traditional methods - UV Persulfate and high temperature thermal.

We weren't entirely excluded. If I remember correctly, there was a short addendum to the standard which mentioned 'some other appropriate oxidation method'. That phrase left the door ajar for us.

But of course, all of our competitors were able to weaponise our exclusion. "Don't go buying a BioTector. Their process is non-standard." Because regulation drove sales, it was easy to scaremonger. "You don't want to be going near something that hasn't been tried and tested."

To say we were underestimated by our competitors is a bit of an understatement. In fact, in 2006, we managed to get hold of a document from one of our competitors – LAR in Germany – in which they analysed each of their competitors' impact on the market. BioTector merited just two words. 'No threat'.

Because most sales in this sector were regulatory sales, analysers were a grudge buy. Typically, the client would spend their budget at the very end of the year.

They'd say, "Right. The EPA is on our backs. We'd better get one of these TOC analysers." They would buy the cheapest and tick the box.

The other point was that because the two legacy technologies were so flawed, everyone hated TOC analysers, and we were tarred with the same brush. When Dad or Seamus went to a conference or an exhibition to do a presentation on BioTector, the negativity would hit them at the door. "We hate these TOC analysers, but we have to buy them." In fact, Dad says that whenever he introduced himself and said that he had a TOC analyser, people would shake their heads sorrowfully and say "I'm sorry for your troubles."

But we could see too that this was an opportunity for us. We were different. We didn't have the horrendous maintenance issues that plagued the other technologies. BioTector didn't need to be opened up and cleaned out every week. That was the message we needed to get out there.

Sales and Marketing

There's quite a bit in our story that's untypical. Most Irish start-ups concentrate on the home market and the UK. Then, if they're successful, they'll think about Europe and the US. But as a result of Tor's efforts, we had a number of distributors all around the world from a very early stage. We were in Japan, Malaysia, Louisiana, Texas and all across Europe. Other than in the US and Germany, none of these distributors sold any more than one or two analysers a year, some even less, but between these and our Irish sales, the pipeline ticked over. Crucially, these sales also allowed us to learn something about the market.

When Dad took over Tor's role, he and Seamus would travel round to small exhibitions where they'd meet other analyser people. Our marketing consisted of a sign propped against the front of the exhibition desk which said 'Distributors Wanted'. Believe it or not, this actually worked up to a point. We'd also get the odd phone call or email from someone who'd heard about our system and was interested in adding it to their catalogue. We would also advertise in technical journals and we targeted distributors of like products. When one of the major manufacturers of TOC analysers, Ionics, discontinued production of their high temperature systems, we approached their distributors and managed to recruit quite a few.

We couldn't fly everywhere and evaluate every distributor, so we created a long, convoluted questionnaire to act as a kind of screening tool. No one would take the time to complete it unless they were serious about distributing our product. We also required all sign-ups to buy one discounted analyser and to come to Ireland for training.

We deliberately chose the distributor model over the agency model. The agent makes the sale and walks away. The distributor maintains the product. Dad knew from his experience with Irish Superior how important maintenance income could be. You were never sure of the sale, but once the sale was made, you knew that there would be ten years of continuous revenue as a result. You can plan with that money, you can hire people. Going this route made the analyser attractive to distributors, and of course, because we were supplying the distributor with the necessary parts, we had a piece of that pie too.

He also had good reasons for not taking on the maintenance business himself. For a start, it was hard work. You're at the beck and call of customers, you need to provide 24/7 cover, you have timesheets to organise and a fleet of cars on the road. He felt that taking on maintenance – other than for a few key clients who provided us with test hubs – would become a distraction. We needed to focus on realising the potential of this great product that we had created. Everything would serve that goal.

The other issue with taking on service business is that you create a two-tier working environment. You need to keep production staff wages competitive but you can't move production to China. Service engineers get paid well and have a car. What do you do when you have a production guy who's built the analyser and is more than capable of servicing it earning a different salary to the guy on the road maintaining it? You end up with a massive turnover in production, and we had great people in production that we really wanted to hold onto.

The model we chose is also attractive to customers because it means they only have to deal with one organisation, and there's an added peace of mind inherent in the fact that he who sells must also maintain. If you've got a lot of kit to buy, the smaller the number of suppliers you have to deal with, the better. Each distributor needs to have a decent bag of tricks so that he can offer promotional deals, discounts and so on.

Most of these distributors weren't really pushing BioTector. They would typically offer a wide variety of systems to a wide variety of industries. If one of their clients happened to need a TOC analyser, the distributor would say, "Yes we have one. Here's the brochure, here's the quote." Our marketing may not have been up to much, but neither was theirs.

The contracts we offered to these distributors were non-exclusive. That was important. We could cancel at any time, and so could they. It was low commitment on both sides. If they sold an analyser, we supported them thoroughly, but we didn't have much marketing material to give them, we didn't have great presentations. In fact, we had no real brand recognition in the marketplace. We actually did a survey back in 2006, asking all our customers what TOC analyser they used. Most didn't mention our company at all. As far as they were concerned, BioTector belonged to the distribution company that installed and maintained it.

Nobody knew who we were.

The Meeting

By mid 2006, we were set to sell ninety analysers, giving us a turnover of around €2m. The pipeline looked good. We were picking up more business from the petrochemical, oil and gas industries overseas, and from the pharmaceutical sector at home. This is what triggered Dad to say, "Right. This is the time to move. Let's make the most of this."

I've read since that typically, a start-up company driven by innovators can often get stuck at this point.

With a good product and a great deal of hard work, you can get to the €2m mark, but without a growth strategy, marketing and a strong management team, progress can sometimes falter. The skillset that got you this far may not get you any further. Either you fail to grow beyond this point, or you overstretch and go bust. Getting a business from €2m to €10m is one of the hardest steps to take. Some companies will get an outside investor or maybe an executive board. Dad saw where we were and began to think about succession.

So he called a meeting with himself and Mom, myself and my two brothers. "Right guys," he said, "Can you all come down next week. I have something to present to you."

We all met up in the canteen in BioTector and Dad summed up the work they had done to date.

"I think there's huge potential here," he said, "but there's a whole load of work to be done in getting out there and realising that potential."

He told us flatly that he was more interested in R&D than flying around the world visiting distributors and customers.

"I'll do a certain amount of it," he said, "but what I'm saying is that I'm giving this job to one of you guys, if you want to do it. If you say no, I'm hiring somebody. Don't come to me in three years and say, 'Geeze, this thing is booming. I want to join up.' Now is the time. I need somebody to help me, and I'd love if any one of you would, or all of you would. But if you don't, I'm going to hire somebody, and once I do that, I'm committing to that person, to grow them and to let them earn shares in the company."

For my older brother Keith, this was outside his area of interest, and he was at a stage in his life where taking this kind of risk did not make sense. Paul was still in college, doing his masters. But for me, the opportunity arrived at exactly the right time.

I'd graduated from the University of Limerick in electronics manufacturing six years earlier, and had then got a job as a service engineer with a company called Emerson. They install automation systems for the pharmaceutical industry. I stayed with them for a couple of years before going out on my own as a contractor. As I sat in the canteen to hear Dad's presentation, my business was going really well. If I was to come into BioTector, I would have to take a substantial pay cut, and sign up for significant amounts of foreign travel.

It's easy to be wise in hindsight, but the truth was

that despite Dad's enthusiasm, there was no guarantee that BioTector was going to make anyone wealthy. There was as much potential for failure as success. As I've said, our competitors were huge. But Dad believed in it, and I could see the potential. Plus I knew my way around factories and engineering. And in an odd sort of way, taking a big salary cut made it feel like no one was doing me a favour. This wasn't Dad giving me the keys to something I hadn't earned. It was an opportunity, but that's all it was. So I said, 'Right, I'll do it.'

Mindset

When I closed up my fledgling company in 2006 and joined BioTector, everyone told me I was mad. The pharmaceutical sector I had been operating in was booming. I think the key reason I shut up shop and came into the business was because it simply felt like an interesting challenge. Dad's enthusiasm for the product was infectious. I was twenty-seven and unmarried – though I was going out with Sue at the time. Really, I just felt that I couldn't say no. And anyway, what was the worst that could happen? If it didn't work out, I could just come back to my old sector and start again.

I grew up in an entrepreneurial household. Mom

and Dad had built Irish Superior Safety Systems into a very successful business, but they had also had numerous other ventures. There was always something new going on in our house. When the Soviet Union opened up, they shipped containers of pharmaceutical supplies to Moscow. My Dad's brother Tom was based over there at the time. Mom and Dad also experimented with buying Soviet street art and bringing it back to Ireland to test the market. I can remember myself and Mom going around shops with a suitcase full of all sorts of things, asking shop owners if they would sell. Neither she nor Dad was ever afraid to take chances.

They had this other thing called Skinstrument. I remember myself and my brother going, "Skinstrument? No one is going to buy something called 'skinstrument'".

It measured the moisture in your skin. You'd take a measurement, use Brand X moisturiser for a month, then measure it again and you'd see how much more moisture your skin retained. The plan was to sell it to the likes of L'Oréal. I think one of the reasons it didn't work was that it turned out that the cheapest moisturiser out there was just as good as the dearer stuff.

The thing was, when these ventures failed, there was never a sense of 'Oh, that was terrible. Why did we do that?' There was never any doom and gloom. It was simply, that was that, now it's done. What's next? We all inherited that mindset. Try it out, give it a go. There's no shame in failure.

Strategy

I joined in September of 2006, on the day of my 28th birthday. On that first day, Dad had scheduled a workshop with Paul from O'Kelly Sutton during which we would establish a strategy for taking this wonderful product and building a wonderful business around it.

It was a baptism of fire.

While Dad and Seamus had been doing a lot of travelling up to this point, Paul O'Kelly argued that we really needed to ramp this up. We had to begin marketing, we had to identify our best distributors, we had to start meeting people at the right level in client companies, we had to stop talking about pumps and valves and start talking about return on investment. It was all a bit daunting because everyone was looking at me. I was thinking, hang on, better have a chat with Sue about this...

When it comes to goal setting, I'm very visual. I don't write goals down. I don't personally find that useful. I visualise them, I see the result in my head. Goals either feel right or they don't. If I work out a goal and it still feels exciting three weeks later, I'll know it's the right thing to go after. It's a gut feeling really. That first strategy session was excellent because it gave me the visual I needed to latch on to.

"At the moment" said Paul, "you go into the client company and you talk technicals to a technical person. You're fighting about pricing. You're talking about pumps and valves. Success for you is that one day, you'll go into Coca-Cola headquarters. You'll be meeting the CEO or the Chief Financial Officer, or maybe the Chief Sustainability Officer. You won't be meeting people wearing overalls anymore. You'll be wearing a suit and the client will be wearing a suit."

The clothes thing always stuck in my mind.

He went on, "You're going to give a compelling presentation to these C-suite executives. You're going to propose the rollout of BioTector across 200 of Coca-Cola's factories and you're going to tell them exactly what the return on investment will be. You'll be talking about increasing their yield, reducing their losses."

"That," he said, "is where you have to get to."

At the time, a single sale could take six months to close. Each one was hard won. We were going into each plant individually. The idea that you would go in at a much higher level and sell multiple units across an entire company was entirely alien.

I suddenly saw – we all saw – that for us to achieve this vision, a lot more than just the sales pitch would have to change. Distributors would have to improve, the production process would have to be streamlined. Any client considering rolling BioTector out across the entire company would want to come and see the factory. They would have to be reassured that it was a professional factory, with proper policies and procedures. Is it ISO compliant? Do you have 5S? Are supply lines and logistics all secure? Smaller clients may have the autonomy to buy whatever analyser they liked, but if you're intent on scaling and getting into bigger organisations, you will need to convince them that you're not going to disappear overnight.

We had a mountain to climb.

While this strategy session did conclude with specific targets, the picture that Paul O'Kelly painted, of meeting Coca-Cola (or an equivalent company) and getting the analyser specified across the entire company, *that* is what stayed with me. With that in mind, over the coming months and years, I would look around and see, ok, there's one reason we can't do that yet. That has to be fixed. And there's another reason. That has to be fixed too. And there's another…and so on.

One point I need to make very clear is that this wasn't all me. Far from it. It was Dad, it was Seamus, it was Ian and Ali and Jayne. It was all of the great people that comprised the BioTector team throughout those years.

Following Dad Around

When I joined, I didn't really know what role to take on. I sat in with the R&D guys and eventually Dad and I agreed that I would project manage the addition of a nitrogen and phosphorus analysis function on the analyser. Project management was something I had some experience of in my old job.

Mainly though, I just followed Dad everywhere. At the time, every single decision went through him. If they were changing anything in the analyser, no matter how small, he had to approve it. So if the ultimate goal was to take over from him, I had to shadow him. I remember during that first week he disappeared one morning – to an Enterprise Ireland meeting I hadn't been invited to. Enterprise Ireland is the government agency responsible for the promotion of Irish export companies. They provided a lot of training and support around this time. When he came back I was there, "You went out? You had a meeting? Without me?" That, I think, brought it home to him exactly what he had taken on. But ultimately, he was ok with that. If the eventual plan was that I should take over from him, I had to know everything. So I moved Dad out of his plush upstairs office into a double one downstairs with me, where I could listen in on all his phone calls and witness all of his interactions. I asked him a million questions, and probably drove him cracked.

The deal we agreed is that I would get a bonus for every ten units we sold over the ninety sold in 2006. This gave me a path back to my old salary. And I suppose it's fair to say that I had the confidence of youth. I had been working in big factories, and if I'm honest, I felt I was stepping down to join a small operation. I thought to myself, *I'll show them how to do things right.*

One of the big shocks was just how much Dad did during the day, and just how deeply involved he was in the tiniest of decisions. Big companies have structures and management teams. From following Dad around, going into every meeting and sticking my head into everything, I found out just how complex the company's operations actually were. And of course on top of that, the product itself was highly complex too, and so too was the production process.

On paper, we had the structures. There was an R&D manager, which was Seamus. There was a production manager, which was Ian. There were others in the company with key responsibilities, but in reality, everything went through Dad. Even if Seamus had run loads of tests, and knew the answer, he'd still go to Dad and say, "We're thinking of changing this valve to this valve, we've run all of these tests. What do you think?" And Dad would have the final say.

Part of that was Dad's own fault. He could have said, "Come on, guys. You're here long enough now. Why am I coming down to look at this?" But he was genuinely interested. This kind of detail was what he loved best. Trying to figure out whether we should change a valve was a nice distraction from marketing, HR, recruitment and invoices. A kind of co-dependency had evolved.

So I found the going tough at the beginning. The whole process was so complicated, there was so much to learn, and yet there was all of this stuff that we weren't doing. I had to try to get to grips with the day-to-day stuff and at the same time work out how we would market and sell and come up with a way of delivering on the potential we knew the product had.

I needed training. This began with a basic sales training course run by Plato Cork. Then I did a second course on international sales which was funded by Enterprise Ireland. That one was absolutely fantastic. It was the first step away from having technical conversations with clients, towards having conversations about value and return on investment.

I learned about finding distributors, managing distributors, how to know what a good one looks like. I learned about marketing, elevator pitches and so on. While these courses took up a lot of time, they were really needed. And I was able to implement based on what I was learning almost straight away.

One thing I realised very soon after I joined the company was that we would have to change our name. There were simply too many names. Pollution Control Systems was selling BioTector via X Distributor. The analyser had BioTector printed on it, but open the door and it said 'Manufactured by Pollution Control Systems'. The other disadvantage of the existing company name was that it identified us too closely with end-of-pipe solutions. The real value of our proposition was back up the pipe, much closer to the production process itself. More – much more – about that later on.

There was no resistance to the name change. We became BioTector Analytical Systems Ltd, or BioTector for short.

The Valve

And I started going out with Dad and Seamus to sales meetings. I said nothing in all of these early meetings, I just sat and watched, trying to sense the mood in the room, trying to get a feel for how things were going. Dad's presentations were both highly technical and highly detailed. I mean highly, highly detailed. One slide might show a valve and in the next one, the valve would have turned by the tiniest fraction. Now, some people love that kind of thing, but I had the sense that because his audience had a lot of respect for Dad, he was being given a fair amount of leeway. The overwhelming feeling was that these presentations were being tolerated rather than appreciated.

There mightn't have been much resistance to changing the name, but there was quite a bit of resistance to changing the presentation. When I suggested cutting back on the detail, Dad would say, "No, no. They absolutely need to know how that valve works. It's critical to the whole thing."

Seamus and all the R&D and production guys agreed. "David," I was told, "You can't not talk about the valve."

So I was kind of stuck. I knew from our strategy session with Paul O'Kelly that we needed to change the story, but the reality was that everyone in the company was so proud of the technology, they wanted to tell the world about the valve.

And my first presentations were awful. I hadn't lived the technology as Dad and Seamus had, so I couldn't get quite as excited about the valve. I could sense too that whatever leeway the founder had gotten, that wasn't going to be extended to me. And when I went out with distributors, I could see that they got even less. The clients were usually too polite to say it but the unmistakeable message was, "What do you want? Whatever it is, tell me quick. I have another meeting in ten minutes."

It actually took a long, long time to get the right presentation. And we were still talking to the wrong people. The problem, of course, was that we didn't have any story for the right people. We couldn't start talking about value or ROI because we didn't know ourselves. We had a technical story for technical people. That was all.

The big question boiled down to this: Where do we take it from here? I was doing the courses, I was travelling, I had a strong sense of where we needed to end up. But not how to get there. In those early days, I was so busy flying around meeting clients and distributors and doing these courses that I was kind of invisible in the office. I knew that what I was doing was essential but at the same time I was bothered about what people in the office thought – or what I thought they thought. I know that succession planning is often handled badly in SMEs. The owner's son or daughter joins the business and the perception among those who've been there for years is that the newcomer is getting something for nothing. Now, nobody ever gave me the impression that they thought this. It was simply a sensitivity that I had.

Part of me wanted to impress the office, but the only way to impress the office was to be an engineer. And the reality was that we didn't need any more engineers, we needed someone to do all of these other vital things, things which attracted less status. I mentioned that when I came in first, I project managed the expansion of the unit's analysis capacity. As part of that project, someone needed to map out the total nitrogen and total phosphorus liquid flows for the software engineer. I decided to take that on as well. It took ages but in the end it was a nice piece of work, and I got some kudos for it. People said, "Nice one, well done."

"Great," I thought. "I'm one of them now."

But in the back of my mind, I knew. This was a waste of time. This was not what I should have been doing. If I was going to make a difference here, I couldn't be one of the engineers. Dad and Seamus had a cult following in the office, but I would never have that, and I had to accept it. I had to do what was right for the business and forget about perceptions or status or any of that.

Chapter 3 – Selling Solutions

Travelling would become a vital part of my education about clients, distributors and the market itself. Going out on these sales trips, living what the sales rep is living, that should be compulsory for all aspiring CEOs.

I'd call up the head of the distribution company and I'd tell them that I was coming over, that I wanted to sit into their meetings and go out and meet our clients. These road trips with distributors were particularly important. When you're locked into the car with someone for hours on a highway, that's when you find out what's going on. Distributors, as I've said, have a range of things on their catalogue. Your product is one of many. And now they have a TOC expert sitting with them in the car. You quickly find out just how comfortable they are with your technology. If they're steering the conversation away from your product, or they're trying to keep it as high level as possible, that's a clear signal that they don't know enough about it.

The Price and The Value
One thing they did know enough about however was the

price, and they weren't slow to complain about it.

"You need to drop your prices." I heard that constantly. "Can you feed that back to Martin? We'd do way more if you dropped your price."

So I'd come home and say, "Dad, I think we need to drop the price."

He didn't want to drop the price any more than he wanted to drop the valve from the presentation.

"We're not dropping the price. We're just not."

He'd had many discussions with customers over the years about the implications of a bad TOC measurement, and was convinced that a reliable measurement could save companies thousands, perhaps hundreds of thousands. There was, he believed, a huge, untapped market out there. To reduce margins now would be to miss that point, and inhibit the financial viability of the company.

Don and Mack shared this view. They believed that this technology was going to become much more important in the years ahead. The regulatory imperative would change. The grudge-buy status would change. And being so much better at the job than our competitors, that would matter. The value was there – people just didn't see it yet.

Mom too was a big believer in holding steady on

price. She prepared monthly management reports which we would sit down and review over a cup of coffee up in her office. She always prioritized data and analysis relating to the actual operation of the business – as opposed to things like depreciation and other non-operational stuff. Our focus tended to be on sales, cost of sales, wages, stock, upcoming orders, distributor performance, R&D spend and so on. The big ones were margin and the average BioTector selling price. She tracked the latter very diligently, placing it at the top of her reports. She always maintained that if we ran a tight ship and avoided any slippage in the unit sales price, everything else would fall into place.

So I would go back to our distributors. "No, sorry, we're not dropping the price."

They'd shrug and say ok, but soon after that, I'd get a call. "You've lost another sale. The price is just too high. Your competitor won it at this price." There was a big 'I told you so' element to all of this. You got the impression that they were almost happy to have failed.

Later in the year, I'd call up and say, "You're not on target for this year, you're supposed to sell four analysers."

They'd tell me, "I'll sell none unless you change

your price."

The Exceptions

But there were exceptions to that. There was a guy in France who was selling, a guy in Germany who was selling, a guy in South Korea who was selling and a guy here in Ireland who was selling. We had loyal customers who did not ask for a lower price.

There's a tendency, when you're busy, to ignore the parts of your business that are doing okay, and to focus instead on the areas that are doing poorly, on the people doing the most complaining. I was responding to callers who said, "You come out here and I'll show you why I can't sell this analyser."

I found myself travelling just to be lectured on the fact that the price was too high. But when I started looking at the successful ones, I made some interesting discoveries. First of all, all of the successful distributors had great relationships with their clients, and all of them were solution focused.

So if the customer said, "I need a sampling system to deliver the sample to the analyser," the distributor would say, "I can do that for you." If the customer said, "I need a house to put it in," the distributor would say, "I can do that for you."

I didn't know it at the time, but of course you've got two types of salespeople. Type 1 is the transactional salesperson. 'I have all this stuff. Here's my catalogue. I'll give you a great discount.' If you have a product that's only slightly differentiated from everyone else's product, you want to get in with a transactional seller and benefit from his relationship with the client. But if you have something that's a bit different and a lot more expensive, you'll never fit with a transactional seller. You give him a product like BioTector and he now has to explain why it's unique, why it's often twice as expensive and what justifies that expense.

Type 2 are the value or solution sellers. They have way less products in their catalogue and are far more solution-focused. They set out to understand what the customer is trying to do, and spend a lot of time coming up with ways of helping them to do it. They enable the sale through these little add-ons, things that a transactional seller wouldn't dream of getting involved in. That adds value for the customer, and makes the higher price worth paying.

A transactional seller puts the entire onus on the

customer to know what he wants. "This is what we have, pick what you want." A solution seller says, "I understand what you're trying to do here, I understand your objectives around bottom line, sustainability and reputation. I know what you're trying to achieve. Yes this product is more expensive but it delivers a solution." A solution seller is on the same side of the desk as the client. He's on the same team. He's there to solve their problems. If he's ready to tailor a solution for them, and has the support of the team and the distribution company behind him, he can then command a high price. This is how you overcome the high price barrier.

I could see that this was the only way to go. This handful of exceptional distributors was prepared to do whatever the customer needed. So I took what I guess was a dramatic step. I cancelled a load of distributors.

New Directions

I say 'I' but really throughout this phase it was me and Dad. We talked endlessly throughout this phase, trying to figure out what it was we were learning from all the travelling, trying to figure out what a good distributor looked like and how we might secure more of them. Cancelling bundles of distributors en masse caused a lot of upset because it meant getting rid of some of our sales. Dad found it particularly hard because he had built up relationships with many of these guys, and some would have been with him from the start. He took quite a few irate calls.

"Are you aware of what David is doing? After all we've been through?"

And Dad would have to say, "Come on. What sales have you been making?"

And we were fair with them. If they had put months into a particular sale, we let them finish it off.

In the meantime, I was lining up new distributors. These were people I'd met at exhibitions, or I might have talked to over the phone. I did a lot of web-based research too. I found out what other products our successful distributors were selling, then looked for distributors in other jurisdictions who were selling the same things. I'd always check how many products they were selling. Was it too many? If I found a distributor I thought might be a good fit, I'd just call them up and talk to them, and we'd start working out a contract. There was a lot of trial and error.

All of these contracts were non-exclusive, meaning either of us could get out at any time. Most wanted exclusivity, but we refused. We would say to them, "We're not giving you an exclusive contract, but we won't put a competitor in against you. If you can sell, you don't have to worry about anything. If you don't sell, we'll be having a different conversation."

A non-exclusive was important, because really, we didn't know what we were doing. We had to be able to get out of the contract if it wasn't working or if we discovered that we'd taken a wrong turn. This requirement meant that some distributors walked away. The really big, dream distributors would never, ever work on a non-exclusive basis. But we were still feeling our way, and there was a mutuality about working with these smaller guys. We needed them and they needed us. All were hovering around the €2 to €3 million turnover mark, and so were we, so it was a well-balanced relationship.

One thing I want to mention at this point. I had always thought of us as well, a *nice* company. We treated everyone well. Our core values, which I'll talk about later, were built around the fact that we were a family company and we always treated customers, suppliers and the people who worked with us fairly. I've realised however, as I began writing our story, that the truth is that we were ruthless with distributors. As I've said, we always had very flexible contracts with them – contracts that allowed either of us to walk away without penalty – but we exercised that right frequently. If we felt that the distributor was a poor match, or wasn't living up to expectations, we cancelled and moved on. I would justify this by saying that we had set out to build and supply the best analyser in the world. To make that happen, every part of the process had to be as good as it could possibly be. If there's a weak link in the distribution channel, you're failing in the commitment you've made to yourself, to your people, to your customers.

Distributors were never that hard to find, and as time went on, we got better at identifying the good ones and the bad ones. That international sales course that I had done shortly after joining the company also covered the management of distributors, and what I learned was really useful. Between us, myself and Jayne (who I'll talk about in more detail later on) implemented a distributor management system.

It worked like this: Every potential sale that a distributor mentioned was logged and tracked. If they talked about an upcoming project that looked a good prospect, we wrote it down. At the same time, we developed a system for characterising a sales process. If a quote goes out, that's stage one. If the distributor goes to see the site and the customer provides application information, that's stage two...and so on up to stage five, at which point the sale closes. Each month, myself and Jayne would phone every distributor and go through this process, checking back on all of the projects they had mentioned the previous month to see how they had progressed, if they had progressed at all. This meant that a distributor could not keep talking about the same projects for two years. If a quote had gone out in January and nothing further had happened by March, it was pretty clear that the sale had been lost. With this system in place distributors could not make vague promises, they couldn't say 'Oh, we'll definitely have three this year', they could no longer fudge the question when we asked them about a particular project. Either it was moving forward, or it was lost. And if a sale was lost, we tracked that too. Why was it lost? What could we do differently the next time?

A few months of this and most distributors fell into line and began giving us more honest and accurate answers. If they felt a project wasn't going to deliver this year, they'd say so.

There were other advantages to this. It allowed us to see who the good distributors were, and who were the not so good. We could introduce new distributors to our tracking system from the very beginning and effectively train them on how to behave. It also helped us to optimise travel. You wouldn't waste time flying out to a distributor who had projects that were going nowhere. Instead, you'd go see those who had more promising prospects, where you could help things along.

Setting Sales Targets

Here was another question we needed to answer. How much *should* our distributors be selling in France, or Germany or Italy? Exactly how big was the market?

We had a good handle on the Irish market, where typically we would sell ten units a year, but how might that translate to other countries? If it's ten in Ireland, what's the equivalent number in Germany? The obvious solution would be to go spend a lot of money on market research. Instead, I spent a lot of time online, and eventually came across something called the European Pollutant Emission Register, which is designed to provide emissions data on both a national and a European level. In order to make it onto the register, a factory has to be of a certain size and it has to be manufacturing something. I was able to look across the sectors which had plants in Ireland, and compare them directly with equivalent sectors in Germany, France, Italy and so on. It was a simple exercise then to extrapolate and see what our ten per year in Ireland would suggest for each of our neighbouring markets. Ok, it wasn't a perfect measure, but it was something we could take to distributors and say, 'Look, this is what you could be doing.' Moreover, we also found that the US had an equivalent list, as did China and Japan.

Soon we had a very good range of distributors all over the world; Germany, Spain, France, Sweden, China, Japan, Malaysia and South Africa, to name a few. Dad and I managed the travelling between us, so that there was always someone keeping an eye on things at home. In between trips we would compare notes, sifting through our shared experiences for valuable nuggets of information.

The great thing about Dad travelling was that when I was in the office, the stuff that usually went through him started coming to me. Everyone was used to getting sign off, but now, when they asked me, I would say, "I haven't a clue. What do you think?"

Invariably, they had the answer to any question they asked, so I'd let them talk me through it and in the end, we'd go with what they felt was the best solution. That process helped to drive the changes we needed to make around reporting lines, responsibilities and how people needed to work.

Downturn

So 2006, the year I joined, we'd done really well, selling nearly 90 units. But in 2007, our sales went down, not up. Part of the issue was my swathe of distributor cancellations, but it wasn't the whole story. The petrochemical, oil and gas industries were our most reliable ordering engines. Next came pharma, then dairy, brewing and other industries. By early 2007, the pipeline was looking particularly good in oil and gas. There was a variety of projects about to break ground; in America, in Saudi Arabia, in Germany, and we were getting commitments to order based on these. But we weren't getting sign off. Every time we'd call up, they'd say, "Yeah, the sale is yours, but we don't have the final signature...I'll look into it, should have it next week."

But next week came and went without a signature. What would emerge over time is that those at the top of the petrochemical, oil and gas industries had some inkling of the recession that was about to hit, and so had drawn in their horns and stopped spending money. So despite the great pipeline, sales slumped to 74 in 2007, and to 63 in 2008.

So much for my bonus.

This was bad, obviously, but we knew it was a

global issue. No one was saying that they didn't want our analyser, they were just saying that they couldn't buy one this year. We also knew we could weather the storm because we were well resourced and, more particularly, we were not overextended. Dad puts it like this, "If we had borrowed money or had financial commitments, we would not have survived. There's no doubt about that." It was always Dad's philosophy to leave money in the company. He maintained that if you didn't keep the money there, you hampered its ability to grow. He says, "With money, you can stand up to your competitors, you can afford to take risks, you can afford to develop." Throughout the property boom, when people were pulling money out of their companies to do all sorts of things, we resisted that temptation.

We had one great distributor in South Korea. He was just one guy working on his own, and because his English was poor, it was really difficult to communicate with him. At the end of 2008, he brought in three new sales, which meant that we just about managed to break even. We could have got away with letting a few production people go at this point, and arguably we should have, but we were still confident in the product and the pipeline and it didn't make sense to lose people if you were only going to have to rehire twelve months later. So we redeployed a few production people to R&D, where there was always something interesting to do. In fact, we were able to use the excess numbers during this quiet time to expedite the move away from transactional and towards value selling.

One of our best distributors was based in Malaysia. I travelled out to him and found that he was doing the same thing as the French guy. The customer would give him a checklist of things he needed, telling him, "If I install BioTector, I'll need this, this and this."

The guy in Malaysia would say, "No problem, we'll look after all of that for you."

So throughout 2007 and 2008, R&D was a hive of activity, developing sampling systems and various other bits and pieces that arose as a result of the needs of the client. And here too was an advantage we could have over the competition. Most of our competitors were big companies with automated production processes who had no interest in adding bells and whistles to their systems. But we, along with the guy in Malaysia and the guy in France, were able to say to our distributors that if sampling issues came up, we had these sampling systems. If the housing issue comes up, we've got this house. We began to build up little additional ways of enabling the sale.

Key Industries

We built a lot of our plans around the petrochemical, oil and gas industries. These were the early adopters, the leaders in this area. Why? For one thing, they're dealing with a very high value product. Losses are costly, so the sooner they know about those losses, the better. More importantly though, the environmental risks of leaks and spillages, and the consequent dangers to reputation are huge. So they had a different mindset to everybody else. For people like Mack and Don, an analyser wasn't a regulatory buy. They took the longer view, and their support gave us huge confidence during the financial crisis. Moreover, we knew that where petrochemicals, oil and gas went, pharma, dairy, brewing and others were sure to follow. All of these industries used huge amounts of water, they had plants full of pipes with liquids flowing over and back. Losses would always be costly. At some point in their journey, they'd need us.

So we told our distributors, "Stick to these few niche areas. Don't bother with dairy. They don't understand it, not really, not yet." We knew that while price was becoming less of an issue with oil and gas, it would still be a major stumbling block in dairy, brewing and so on. So the strategy here was wait and see.

Adding Value

Now too, we began to see a little more clearly how we could define the ways in which the analyser could add value. The inspiration for this came, as before, from Mack and Don.

So far, the only place you would put your TOC analyser was right at the end of the pipe, after the treatment plant, just before you discharge into the water course. You want to make sure there's nothing in there that will cause any environmental issues. This means that most of the time, the quality of liquid flowing into the analyser is pretty good.

But what if you also had an analyser, or analysers, back up the line, at earlier stages of the production process? Could they provide you with useful information, when the liquid flowing through is dirtier? This wasn't a question you could ask of either of the two traditional TOC technologies, because those analysers just couldn't handle anything other than clean, or almost clean liquid. Oil or particulate matter choked them up instantly. But because ours was self-cleaning and could tolerate pure oil or pure milk flowing through it, this was a question you could validly ask. Suppose you installed an analyser *just before* rather than just after the treatment plant. If you knew the levels of pollution coming in, then perhaps you could turn down the blowers to reduce the levels of aeration, and so save energy. Could you also optimise the amount of chemicals needed to treat the waste?

Now, at last, we could think about constructing an argument in which BioTector wasn't a grudge buy, it was a want buy. BioTector could save you money.

Ohmart VEGA

Despite the great relationship we had with Mack and Don, we'd never had a distributor big enough to cover the whole of the US. That changed in 2007 when we signed Ohmart VEGA. They were the first big distributor that approached us, the first big distributor we signed. They were an amalgamation of Ohmart – an American firm, and VEGA, who were German, and they sold substantial volumes of equipment into the oil and gas industry. At the time, we had three distributors in America – in Louisiana, Ohio and Texas. Ohmart VEGA would replace all three. This was a really exciting deal. We were sure that they would unlock not alone oil and gas, but a wide range of other industries as well. They had a turnover in the hundreds of millions. A far cry from all of the other distributors we'd been dealing with up to that point.

But it wasn't a case of just signing them, agreeing a level of sales and off we go. To make the most of this opportunity, we had to bring a lot more structure to our processes. Our ordering system in particular had to change. With all our other distributors, we told them what to do. They'd fax in an order – frequently handwritten – and we started producing. Not anymore. Our whole ordering system had to be revamped and standardised. The production manager had to establish a system which could take in an order and deliver exactly as Ohmart required. As it happened, our production manager, Ian, was perfectly suited to this role. He always hated the ad-hoc way in which orders came in and were filled. He threw himself into the professionalisation of the process and did a wonderful job. He was like, "Finally! This is exactly what I've been looking for." We started acting like a big company instead of a small company.

Ohmart were solution sellers. They had what I'd call a top down/bottom up sales process. Just as we had always done, they went into the client at quite a low level and talked to the treatment plant manager or the maintenance people about how BioTector worked and what a great piece of kit it was. But they would also go in at a higher level and try to connect with people who had a broader remit, who might have responsibilities that went beyond treatment and maintenance. The aspiration was that these two conversations would somehow meet in the middle and quicken the sale.

Adapting to this new approach meant we had to do some serious work on our sales presentation. It had to be shorter, more impactful, less technical and easier to understand. Myself and Dad used to feedback to each other about how each presentation had gone, noting which slides got a reaction and which didn't. We were continually tweaking things. There were several versions of the slide deck in circulation, and we'd pick one depending on the audience. More technical for those in overalls, more value oriented for those in suits.

And I was still going on those extended car trips with reps, which I still found exceptionally useful. With all of the other distributors, I'd spend a lot of time explaining the system to them. Without actually telling them their job, I'd be giving the kind of information which I hoped would enable sales. With Ohmart VEGA however, the knowledge flowed in the opposite direction. There was one particular guy – Ron Bridges – that I travelled with. He knew far more than I did about selling in general and about solution selling in particular. He helped me to refine the sales presentation. He was great too at gauging the feeling around the table and interpreting reactions to what we were saying.

Because they were solution sellers, Ohmart didn't simply add BioTector to the catalogue. They spent a lot of time understanding the product and scripting their sales pitch. They identified the issue we'd always had with the slide deck. A technical presentation of some kind was necessary but it was really difficult to make it concise, comprehensive and engaging. Their solution? Ohmart spent $15,000 developing an animated video that clearly showed the movement of liquid through the different parts of the analyser. This revolutionised the technical side of the sales pitch, and gave us a lot of confidence that they would be there for the long haul.

They also needed a lot of service training, and this is where Ali Demir's training and technical support abilities came to the fore. He put a huge effort into service training presentations and trouble-shooting guides, making them concise and clear, so that as many engineers as necessary could be brought through training as quickly as possible.

Sometimes, the customer would buy an analyser for the usual end-of-pipe reasons, and like it so much that they would want another to be installed at an earlier stage in the production process. This was great in principal because we knew that's where we wanted to be ultimately, but clients never had the budget for these experiments. We would usually agree to a trial for a set period, with a sliding discount scale so that the earlier they decided to buy, the cheaper it would be. These demos were always a pain in the ass. You didn't want the analyser back because you couldn't sell it to anyone else, but in the back of your mind you're curious about why they're using it where they're using it and what they might find out. So whenever a distributor came through with a demo request, we would usually agree, but tell the distributor to keep a close eye on the installation and find out as much as possible about it. And if a sale followed, we were always keen to go back and discover what it was that justified spending forty grand.

Ohmart helped us to formalise this process, and turn it into a powerful sales tool by setting out application notes for these demos. *This is the benefit to the customer of this installation; this is why no other analyser can perform this function.* Ohmart may not have been able to put figures on it, but they were approaching the return on investment argument that remained the Holy Grail. They had marketing people who could take these application notes and create a story around them. This work would be hugely beneficial to us in the years that followed.

And throughout the relationship, Ohmart were extremely good to us. They were unusual in that they were a big company that behaved like a small family company. They were honourable, they had a lovely culture – you'd feel it when you walked through their factory in Cincinnati. So there was a great fit between us.

But in the end, none of it worked. We thought Ohmart VEGA would be selling 200 analysers in the states alone. So did they. But it never happened. The sales never came. By mid 2009, the relationship was over.

On paper it looked perfect. They were deeply involved in the oil and gas industry, and had a particular specialism in gauges for oil tanks and non intrusive ways of measuring levels and things like that. But it would turn out that while they were in the right industry, they were in the wrong *part* of that industry. They just didn't get water analysis, they didn't get total organic carbon analysis, and in particular, they didn't get just how much effort went into a sale.

They tried, they tried really hard. They were brilliant to work with and we got on great with them.

Everything was perfect from that point of view. But they just didn't get that part of the industry. We were dimly aware that there might be a mismatch, but they were such a big organisation with so many salespeople and such a great brand that we thought they'd figure it out. *They* thought we'd figure it out.

Here was an important lesson. There are niches, then there are niches within niches. Nor did it help that they came on board in the middle of a recession. I mentioned that sales slumped to 63. In 2009, they fell to 59.

The end came when the VEGA part of the company bought out the Ohmart part. They called us up to say that they didn't see the fit with BioTector anymore. "We're really sorry about this but we're going to have to cancel the agreement."

Chapter 4 – An Offer and a New Deal

It was a blow. Myself and Dad had invested huge amounts of time flying around getting the sales side up and running. Much of the service training work had fallen to R&D because nobody knew the analyser better than them. This was more wasted effort, and now too we would have to go back to the start with a new US partner.

But there were many positives. Our order processing had been overhauled, our sales presentations were much closer to what they needed to be and our service training materials and processes were way better. These improvements had an immediate positive impact on all of our distributors and critically, they demonstrated just how capable Ali and Ian were.

So we all learned a great deal. We were still a small company but now we were acting much more like a big company. And our belief in the ultimate success of BioTector never really wavered. Certainly not Dad's anyway. He totally believed and I believed Dad.

By late 2009, we were emerging from recession and some of the petrochemical, oil and gas projects that had been stalled for the previous two years finally began to get funding. I think too that we weren't hit quite as hard by the recession because we had such geographic diversity. It's unusual for the entire planet to be at the same point in the economic cycle, so while things were still quiet in the US and the UK, distributors in Japan, Malaysia and the Middle East were ordering analysers. Something good was always happening somewhere.

The other advantage in having a global spread is that specific events in individual countries can often operate in your favour. One year, the Taiwanese government brought in a new environmental regulation. We'd had a distributor there who never did much more than one analyser a year. Now suddenly, we had a flood of orders. If we hadn't had that distributor in place to take advantage of that, we would never even have heard about the regulation. There were several of these idiosyncratic demand spikes throughout my time at BioTector.

Enter Hach

The big downside of the Ohmart VEGA cancellation was the fact that we now had no distributor in the US. We put the word out, through Mack, Don and anyone else we knew over there, letting them know that while Ohmart VEGA may be gone, we were still open for business.

Then we got a call from Hach.

A huge, multinational American company, they had always been a competitor. Their product was called Astro and we hated it. It was a UV persulphate analyser, a technology that had been pioneering back in the eighties. But it required constant maintenance and its results were mistrusted by customers. So it was one of the main reasons why everyone hated TOC analysers. Despite all this, Hach had been very successful selling it. It was everywhere.

One of their guys asked if he could come and see us. We agreed of course, so he flew to Ireland to meet up and talk about the analyser. It would turn out that Hach had been following our progress for years. We were told that they could see that we were doing something different, something worth keeping an eye on.

He mentioned acquisition. Possible acquisition. We were flattered by the attention, and said, well, make an offer. So they did some due diligence and came back with a number. €2.65 million. We were highly insulted. That's what they think of our company? How dare they.

Dad got on the phone to them. "Are you missing a zero?"

"We think you're a great company," the guy said, "and we'd really like to buy you at that price."

When our accountant Adrian was in shortly after this, we told him the story of the insulting offer, expecting him to be as outraged as we were. He wasn't.

"Sales have been falling for the past two and a half years," he said. "Based on your turnover, that's pretty much what you're worth."

That was an eye opener.

Dad and Mom however saw the opportunity in this. The value was nowhere near what we hoped it would be, so this was the time to change the share structure of the company. They decided to divide it into thirds. One for them, one for me and one to be divided up between my two brothers. They also formalised a share bonus structure for Seamus in addition to his existing shareholding. At Dad's insistence, this was to come from his and Mom's third. Because the value of the company was low at this point, handing out shares would not generate substantial tax liabilities for the recipients. Dad said, "We're going to knock the socks off this thing in the next few years. Now is the time to distribute before the value elevates the tax liability."

I want to stress that this was all Mom and Dad's decision. Up to this, we'd never talked about succession in terms of ownership. We knew that if all went to plan, Dad would retire and I would take over, but I had neither asked for nor expected that much of the company. That said, I was hugely grateful.

Hach as Distributor

So we told Hach thanks but no thanks.

They said, "Ok, fair enough. How about we look at a distribution partnership instead?"

That was an idea worth exploring.

Hach is owned by a company called Danaher and Danaher is massive. They have a turnover of nearly $20 billion a year. The name isn't so well known because they tend to acquire companies with strong brands which they then retain.

Though both myself and Dad knew that taking on Hach as a distribution partner would be a huge opportunity for the company, there was a lingering bad taste over the poor valuation. This was despite the accountant's reassurance that there was nothing to be insulted about. We just had to get over that and get on with things. Hach had made it clear that they wanted an exclusive contract in both the US and Europe. Because we were already doing pretty well in Europe on our own, we were less enamoured of this idea. We were also getting mixed reports about what the company was like to deal with. In the US, Hach's main focus was the municipal sector. They had few industry customers. By contrast, Hach Lange – which is the name they traded under in Europe – was deeply involved in industry. All of the positive things we heard about Hach came from people who'd had experience of Hach Lange. By contrast, all of the negative things we heard about them related to the American side of the business.

The trip to Colorado for the contract negotiations was a disaster. Our baggage got lost in transit, so when we arrived out to the hotel Hach had booked for us, we had to go back out and buy toothbrushes, clothes, everything. Then that night, a train came through every hour on the hour and blew its horn.

We already had a bad mind for Hach. Now I was lying awake thinking, "This is how they negotiate? Is this the type of people we're dealing with?"

And in the morning, when we came in exhausted and told them what had happened, there was a bit of sniggering around the table. They had known about the train. So had they done it on purpose? In the months and years that followed, there were a lot of trips back out to Colorado but no one was ever put up in that hotel again.

Solution Sellers

Hach were like Ohmart Vega in that they were solution sellers. Unlike Ohmart, Hach were deeply involved in water. So far so good. The problem however was the aforementioned lack of expertise in US industry. They had no real presence in petrochemicals, oil and gas and so were missing one of the three boxes we would have liked to tick.

They sold primarily to government and municipal buyers, mainly wastewater treatment plants run by local authorities. This was a sector we avoided because everything happens very slowly, and the cheapest analyser is always favoured. We did have analysers in a few local authorities in Ireland, but only because we knew them. Everywhere else, we told our distributors to stay away from them.

It would turn out that one of the reasons Hach approached us was because by this stage, we were strong in industry, which they were now targeting. They saw us as a kind of Trojan horse. Get into the plant with BioTector and then start talking about all the other products they had to offer. It was also clear that seeking a distribution deal with us was their Plan B all along. They were completely open about that.

We asked them, "Why go after industrial? Your speciality is municipal, you're great at that. Why change?"

They explained that they'd more or less maxed out on municipal. They had been so successful that there was nowhere left to go. The only growth option therefore was to move into a totally new sector, and of course we fitted neatly with that strategic direction.

We were small, but it would be wrong to think that we were without bargaining power. We had a well proven, patented technology with a very impressive customer list; Exxon Mobil, Dow Chemicals, BASF, Shell, Coca-Cola, Pepsi, Pfizer – all companies that Hach had targeted as they expanded out of the municipal space. We'd earned the right to be here.

The one big concern we had was that Hach was still technically a competitor. They still had this Astro product, which, as I've said, we hated because it did so much reputational damage to TOC analysers. And Hach had no plans to retire the Astro even if they signed us.

We asked them, "How can you continue to offer this product, when the whole rationale behind selling BioTector is that everything else in the market is inferior. You would be speaking out of both sides of your mouth."

Astro, as I say, was a UV Persulfate technology. Hach also had a high temperature analyser on their books. They rationalised their approach by saying, "We can say to the client that we have all three TOC technologies. If you want high temperature, we've got that, if you want UV persulfate, we've got that, but in our opinion, BioTector is the best."

The potential problem with that approach was that it made selling BioTector dependent on the salesperson. If he or she said, "We've all three technologies and BioTector is the best", the client could point out that it was twice the price. What's to stop the sales person saying, "Ok, fine, take the Astro."

A related concern was that we would be giving Hach access to our technology. We did have the patent, but the patent didn't cover everything. There was also that range of components that we'd sourced around the world. Theoretically, it would be very easy for them to say, 'Look, that's a Maxon motor, that's a Watson Marlow pump head. Let's buy them and put them into the Astro.' They could go to all of our suppliers, buy the parts, stick them into the Astro and make it a vastly superior product. That was a risk.

Having said that, the patent was a great source

of comfort. We wouldn't have considered signing the contract without it. And we knew too that UV persulfate was still a flawed technology, and critically, if they did set out to replace key components with much better ones, that would drag the price of their unit much closer to ours.

We were bothered too by the imbalance. Hach were huge, we were tiny. We risked getting entirely swamped by them. If their ambitions – our ambitions – were realised, they would sell hundreds of analysers. We would become wholly dependent on them, lost in them. How do we keep a sense of ourselves in that context?

The Deal

Negotiating with Hach was very different to negotiating with Ohmart VEGA. Ohmart, as I've said, always tried to maintain the small company atmosphere. Hach was a machine. A large, highly driven, highly profitable machine, with a turnover of $2 billion. Ohmart had that family feeling. *We'll figure it out, we'll do right by you.* With Hach, you knew you were dealing with the big boys.

That morning, there were different people mandated to negotiate different elements of the contract. So you'd spend an hour or two with one guy and then he'd disappear and someone else would come in to talk about the next thing.

Typically, we would specify a list price to charge customers and give distributors a 40% discount on that. It was a big discount, but it reflected just how much work went into each sale. So when a distributor sold a unit, they did as well as we did, and that's how we liked it. We wanted to work as much as possible with value sellers and keep the margins high for everybody. We offered the same terms to Hach, along with a couple of additional sweeteners. A 45% discount if they sold over 60 units and 50% if they sold more than 100.

Hach came at us from a number of different angles. First it was purchasing power. They said, "We're Danaher, we're a $20bn company. I'm sure you're paying way more for your raw materials than we are. I bet if we went into your factory, we could identify items that we could get for much better prices." They made out that if we bought something for €100 and they could get it for €50, then we could split the difference.

Next it was R&D. They said, "Let's share our expertise in water and do some joint R&D projects. Together, we could develop some great new products." They had something they called Danaher Business Systems, or DBS, which they described as a well-oiled tool. "We'll come in and help set up your stores for you. There are loads of things we can help you to do much better than you're doing at the moment, and we're happy to share that with you as our valued partner." While DBS was their IP, they assured us that we'd be able to arrive at a mutually advantageous deal.

Myself and Dad had to keep coming out of the meeting room so we could talk these things over privately. It seemed to us that Hach were trying to gain all the advantages of an acquisition without actually paying anything. Our instinct was that this was their way of getting their claws into us and sapping our independence. As far as our purchasing was concerned, we were pretty sure that it was already really good. And of course we had great faith in our own R&D. We knew too from the Ohmart VEGA experience that any contract we might sign could easily be cancelled out of the blue. Where would that leave us if all of our supply lines were routed through them or we had joint IP tied up in new products?

We didn't want to be rude, so we said, "Thanks, thanks very much, that's fantastic but I think maybe we'll just keep it simple for now. Do a standard contract and we'll see how we all get on..."

Normally, payment happens within thirty days of

delivery. We were told that instead of this, we'd be paid immediately, on credit card. This sounded great, but it was unusual, so we rang Mom up and asked her to go check with the bank and see what immediate payment on credit card entailed. It turned out that it entailed a 2% charge, which more than ate up the advantage in getting paid early. If we hadn't got Mom on the case, we would have signed on those terms and only discovered after the fact that they were actually worse. When we pushed back on this, Hach would not agree to the standard 30 day payment, and in the end, we had to settle for 45 days.

The forty-four

We were aware that as far as the US was concerned, we didn't have much bargaining power and couldn't make massive demands. With the end of the Ohmart VEGA contract, we no longer had any distributor in the US and nor did we have any Plan B if the current negotiation didn't work out. Well, we did talk about a plan B. It involved setting up a US office, but this would have been complicated and cumbersome and no one had any enthusiasm for it.

Europe was different. Our existing distributors were selling 44 units a year. If we were to cancel them all and sign with Hach, we'd immediately drop from 44 sales to zero. What if Hach only sold 24 units in the first year? Or less?

We said, "We can't cancel on our friends and valued partners across Europe and take a hit of €500,000 into the bargain. If you can guarantee the value of 44 units, we'll give you the contract for the US and Europe."

We knew this was a big ask. We also knew that the people we were dealing with wouldn't have the authority to sign off on something like this. And if we hated the idea of opening up our purchasing to them, they hated the idea of signing up to the kind of penalty clause we were looking for.

Throughout the two days we were over there, the negotiation kept getting stuck on this. We would go off and talk to one guy about service and agree a deal, then come back to the penalty clause and remain stuck. Then we'd talk to the sales team and agree something with them, then come back again to that penalty clause and again fail to make progress.

It wasn't easy to hold that line, because Hach had the power to really make things happen, to realise the vision that Paul O'Kelly had planted in my mind at that first strategy session. Hach had the status and the capacity to get us into Coca-Cola at the right level and get BioTector specified across the company. Hach had people that would make the transaction sale, but they also had a team that went in at a much higher level to make the value sale. They had a two tier approach, with the emphasis very much on the latter.

Terry was the name of the guy who was leading the negotiation from their side. Eventually, on the evening of the second day, he came in and offered a guarantee for forty sales *in total* – not solely across Europe. This was good enough. We took it. So now we knew we were protected. We had a highly motivated distributor in the states, intent on using BioTector to break into industry. And we had our ideal distributor in Europe, one with an excellent record in industry. It was a five year contract, which meant that even if there was a massive recession, the value of those 40 analysers was guaranteed. The other benefit to us was of course that it signalled that Hach was deadly serious. They wanted to make a go of things.

One final issue with the European market is that we had a number of really outstanding distributors with whom we'd been working closely for some time. We didn't want to see them left high and dry by this new arrangement, so we asked Hach to reach out to them to see if they could come to some kind of mutually beneficial agreement. Thankfully, Hach agreed to do this. And they also acceded to our request to keep Ireland out of the arrangement. We had a lot of test sites at home, plus a really good distributor who was teaching us a lot about the market. More about him later.

We'd also managed to sign a deal without any of those niggly little extras that they'd tried to push on us. The only tricky condition for us was that there would be penalties if the delivery time on a TOC analyser exceeded four weeks, and six weeks for a TOC nitrogen and phosphorus analyser. So we were really going to have to get our shop in order.

There was one other clause in the Hach contract that would become significant a few years later. If a third party came in and made an acceptable acquisition offer, Hach would get first refusal at that price. Given the amount of work they would put into the relationship, you couldn't really object to this. If someone were to sweep in and buy us out, that entire investment would disappear. This is the price of success. You can keep things at arm's length with a smaller distributor but if you want to take it to the next level, if you want to sell hundreds of analysers, you do have to give up certain freedoms.

We came out of Hach that day giddy with excitement. I vividly remember driving out of the car park with the Rocky Mountains away to our west. There was a huge sense of achievement. We knew this was massive.

A New Beginning

With the Hach contract signed, our next priority was getting everyone in BioTector on board and motivated to make the most of this opportunity. This would not be easy. Over the previous three years we had signed distributors throughout Europe, the Middle East and Asia, not to mention Ohmart VEGA in the US. We had all put huge work into training, supporting and developing relationships with each and every one of these.

Now, we were asking the team to dig deep once more and start the process all over again. We would have to train Hach's sales and service teams throughout Europe and the US. We would have to forge new relationships with a whole new set of people. We would also have to brace ourselves for a lot of unhappiness among our cancelled European distributors. All of this would have to happen at the same time and as soon as possible. This was a big ask.

Along each step of the way, we'd put in a lot of time developing distributor relationships, doing all the sales and service training. The way that work pays off, if you do it right, is that you attract the likes of Hach – a company that wouldn't come near you early in the journey. But on the ground, changing over to Hach meant unravelling so much of the great work we had done up to that point.

So while there was some excitement over signing Hach back at BioTector, there was also a sense of 'Oh God, not again'. We needed to get people motivated, we needed to explain to them that this was the big one, that all of the work we'd done, even if it felt like wasted effort, had lead us to this point.

Don't let perfect get in the way of better. All of these changes we made along the way, they made us so much better at what we did. Often, it was two steps forward, one step back, but the key point is that we were getting better all the time, and with each step, we came closer to being able to land the distributor that could really make things happen. And when your dream distributor comes along, you want to be at your best. Thankfully, we were in a position to support Hach much more effectively than we'd ever supported any other distributor before.

Succession

Succession was one more thing we needed to sort out in

advance of Hach's arrival. A lot had been done in this area, but the Hach contract directed our attention back on Dad's involvement and his desire to begin to step back from the business. Taking on all of the inevitable travel would have been a big step in the wrong direction for him. By now people had started coming to me with queries and sign-off, even when Dad was in the office. I was still going to courses and reading tons of books about growing the business. One thing that kept coming up in all of these courses and all of this reading was the vital importance of clear responsibilities and making decisions at the correct level. If Dad was off and I was in Colorado or somewhere, we couldn't have a situation where nobody could make a decision. The office couldn't be allowed to grind to a halt just because we weren't there. On paper, our structures and job titles were right, it was the behaviour of those that held the titles that needed adjustment. We needed to establish ownership and responsibility in each department.

So I said to Dad, "I want to do a strategy session with the team. And if you don't mind, could you not be in the room?"

I had to get the message across to everyone that we could not rely on Dad so much. He'd done his shift in BioTector, he'd put everything into it, built this wonderful company and now it was time for us to step up and take it to the next level. I didn't want Dad there because if he was, everyone would be waiting for him to tell them what the strategy was, and so it would become Dad's strategy. And if it failed, well, it was Dad's strategy. It couldn't be Dad and Mom at that meeting, it had to be just me.

I decided too that rather than getting in a consultant to lead things, we would confine the session to just ourselves. I felt strongly that however the strategy ended up, it had to come from us. It couldn't be Dad's strategy, or Paul O'Kelly's strategy, or even my strategy. It had to be *ours*. I called Paul and talked to him about this idea, and in fairness to him, he endorsed the approach and gave me some pointers about running the session.

As I say, I'd been reading a lot of books, and the one I settled on to help us frame our strategy was 'Mastering the Rockefeller Habits' by Verne Harnish. It's all about cutting through the complications and creating a simple, one page strategy that everyone can understand and implement.

I bought the book for everyone who would be coming to the strategy workshop, and asked them to read it in advance. Like a lot of Irish people, some found it hard to get past the American corniness that you get in books like these.

"Just ignore the over the top stuff," I said, "and take the main points out of it."

I actually bought the book for everyone in the company. I never insisted that everyone read it but I thought it might help them to understand what we would be asking of them when the strategy was settled.

The Strategy

So we booked a room in a hotel and on the day, I stood up and reminded everyone where we had come from, where we were at that moment and how we now had the opportunity to realise our potential. We had developed the best TOC analyser in the world, and were too good a company to be stuck on our current sales figures. I told them that Dad was going to be stepping back and that we needed to facilitate that.

I was brutally honest with myself and with the team. I said that I wasn't Dad. I wasn't as good as him and I wasn't going to try to be him. And in any case, the potential before us couldn't be realised by one individual or even two individuals. We would need a well functioning team. Our production manager would now have to manage production, our R&D manager would have to manage R&D, our store manager would have to manage stores and so on. All decisions appropriate to that level of management would have to be taken there. If you're having trouble, I said, I'll help. If you need to go on a course, we'll organise that. If you're struggling in an area, we can get a consultant in.

As we got into the nitty gritty, I made sure to sit among everyone as much as possible. I wanted the whole thing to be a collaboration. I didn't want to be standing up and doing all the writing.

There was a great deal of positivity around. We looked at all the reasons behind our success. I asked them, "How had we achieved a €2m turnover? Why did we enjoy such a great reputation?

Someone would say, "Our first analysers are still running perfectly after fifteen years."

Someone else would say, "Our technical support is fantastic."

People talked about how our analyser was the best in the world, how we developed bespoke solutions for our customers, about the six month service, about our unique understanding of difficult applications.

These things were always there, but no one had ever articulated them before. It was a fantastic experience, to hear people say why we were as good as we were. I said earlier that we had always had a definable if unstated culture. This was the first time we actually stated it, the first time we said, 'This is who we are'. It was a chance for us to show off, to say look at what we've done. We're tiny compared to our competitors, but look how good we are, look how far we've come.

Product Leadership

One of the key decisions we had to make centred on what kind of company we were. There were three choices. The first was customer intimacy, the second, operational excellence and the third was product leadership. We debated them all but settled ultimately on product leadership. In many ways, we did tick the customer intimacy box, particularly when it came to customer support, but after a lot of back and forth, we realised that that focus was really there to serve the ultimate goal – the original goal – which was to build the best analyser in the world. We were a product leadership company. We will try to be as slick and efficient as we can, and we will try to get our prices as competitive as possible but really nothing trumps product leadership.

From there, we discussed and ultimately named

our core values:

- Six months service
- 100% customer satisfaction
- Innovative solutions/never give up
- Seek perfection through continuous improvement
- Culture of learning
- Honesty for all stakeholders, personal touch to business

We had these core values made up into posters and put up all around the factory. We agreed the actions that flowed from these core values, we discussed which markets were best for us, and how we were going to win in those markets.

One thing that emerged as very important during the strategy session was that no matter what happened with Hach, we could not allow ourselves to turn into them. We would retain a sense that this was a family business. We were very aware that we would have to fight to keep that focus and not get consumed by this enormous company.

Our focus was product leadership, but Hach, by contrast, were more of an operational excellence company, which means they executed very, very well. The way they took orders and shipped was highly streamlined, and they would naturally try to impose that same philosophy on us – hence the penalty clause for late shipping. For us, having slick processes was a priority, but it was not more important than product leadership. We couldn't lose focus on that, we couldn't allow the relationship to dilute the essence of who we were. Product leadership had been instrumental in getting us this far, and we trusted that it was going to get us further.

There was a flexibility inherent in that which small companies lose as they get bigger. You naturally become more operationally focused and lose these wonderful and clever ways you can help your customer.

There were six of us in the room, and over the course of that two days, everyone had their say. Someone would suggest something, someone else would disagree and we'd chat it out until we settled on a solution. I'd say that the strategy we ended up with wasn't brilliant. If we had brought Paul O'Kelly in, it would probably have been better, but it did have one crucial ingredient, and that was buy-in. We did it together and everyone agreed that it was the way to go. That brought a real unity of purpose to the organisation.

Dealing with the four week lead time was a particular issue of course, so I sat down with our production manager, Ian, and decided that we would need to implement Lean Manufacturing. We knew from the Ohmart VEGA experience and the way he had implemented change at that time that Ian was perfectly positioned to drive this initiative.

Likewise, people like Ali and Jayne became even more effective after the strategy session. It was, I think, very liberating for them. Like so many of us, these were people who didn't want to be told what to do, they wanted to be given the challenge and the freedom to tackle it in their own way. They embraced their new responsibilities, and saw them as a means of growth, of forwarding their own careers.

Chapter 5 – Take Off

Believe it or not, up to this point, one person built the entire analyser from start to finish. Nothing left the factory that wasn't 100 per cent, but each one was unique. In fact, if you knew what you were looking for, you could nearly tell when you opened the door of the unit – 'Rob built that one', or 'That's Brendan's, he built that.'

That would have to change.

To be successful with Hach, we needed to take production a lot more seriously. Throughout our history, we had been, as I've said, an R&D company with a bit of production on the side. With these four and six week lead times, as well as the potential for huge orders, getting manufacturing wrong would have a devastating impact on the company.

We had to recognise that actually, R&D is a cost centre. Production is a revenue generator. Production paid R&D's salaries. We clarified the vital importance of the production manager's job to everyone in the company.

Lean Manufacturing & Stock

There was a grant available, which we took advantage of,

and I got a consultant in to help, but it was our production manager Ian O'Mahoney who took charge of implementing Lean Manufacturing.

The manufacturing process was broken down into stations. One station did their bit, then passed it on to the next. It was effectively a push system; when one man was finished, he pushed his part on to the next station so they could get their bit done. It wasn't quite an assembly line but it was modelled along those lines.

Not everyone in production liked this approach, for obvious reasons. It wasn't as flexible for one thing. The guy that built the whole analyser could pick his own time to go and have a cup of tea. With an assembly process, you have to regularise breaks to keep the whole thing moving smoothly and to avoid logjams. Ian did a lot of training in this area, progressing through the different coloured belts that represent the successive certifications in Lean Manufacturing. And he also implemented 5S –a well-known Japanese methodology for organising and streamlining work spaces.

We also took a closer look at our stock. 'Just in time' is the accepted wisdom here. You only maintain enough to keep your processes turning over. We did the opposite and ordered a huge load of parts and components.

We didn't know how successful Hach was going to be, but if they were, we would need to rapidly increase production, and our stocking levels would have to support that. Some of the parts we used were single source. The optical component of the CO_2 analyser, for example, could only be bought from one manufacturer. What if their plant blew up or got flooded? We bought about five years worth of that component. With other parts, there might be two to three different sources, but their lead times were slow. Switching between them could take eight weeks or more. We evaluated the risks associated with each supplier and wrote a lot of cheques to make sure that our shelves were as full as they needed to be. We knew that this was a risk, spending hundreds of thousands on things that you hope will be ordered down the line. But it was also a statement of intent. We had secured our dream distributor, the one that held out the possibility of realising all the great potential we knew we had, and we couldn't mess it up by acting like a small business that couldn't deliver in time.

Research and Development

I mentioned in the first chapter that there are two types of TOC analyser. An online unit caters for the continuous analysis market, where a fluid is passing through a pipe and is tested continually. There's also laboratory analysis, in which a standalone, offline unit tests a sample. On the back of the success of our online analyser, we wanted to see if we could develop a lab analyser using the same technology. But now, as a result of our new strategy, R&D was continually dragged away from this work by a range of supporting roles in other departments.

Calibration, for example. Once production was finished, the unit went to calibration for testing. This is where you pick up any defects or component failure. The problem – as far as streamlining processes goes – is that when something went wrong in calibration, the guys in calibration usually wouldn't know how to fix it. Given the time, they'd figure it out, but we didn't have the time anymore. The only people in the company who could solve problems quickly were those in R&D, so we had to tell them, 'If calibration calls, you drop everything and run.' This wasn't seen as a positive development by R&D. Up to now, they called the shots, they were the innovators, they told everyone else what do to. But now production was the priority. We had to get the analysers out on time. We tried to turn this into a positive for R&D. If something is going wrong in calibration, then try to figure out why. Turn that curiosity, that creativity on the issue. Is there a flaw somewhere? Maybe every 100th component that comes in from a particular supplier is warped or the wrong size.

A vital part of our strategy involved moving the analyser further and further up the pipe, deeper and deeper into the production process. We needed to demonstrate the potential benefit to the customer of deploying BioTector in unexpected places, and it fell to R&D to do the testing that would help to prove that business case. So a customer would ask 'How do I know you can measure this stuff reliably?' I'd say, 'Send over a sample and we'll test it in R&D.'

Next thing, twenty bottles of horrible, foul smelling liquid would arrive over, and I'd explain to R&D that if we could prove that our unit can test these without clogging up, we would have five sales on the back of it. R&D would then have to test each one and prepare a report for the customer. This may not have been the cutting edge work they were used to, but, as I continually pointed out, it was an enabler of success, and had to be seen as such. At the same time, Ali in customer support also began to call on R&D to support his work. Because analysers were now being deployed in different environments, issues tended to arise more frequently, and so the R&D team needed to help out.

So we had to row back on the lab analyser and say, 'Sorry, you've got to prioritise production and sales.' This was hard to manage. But when it paid off and we did get the five sales, it was always very important to say, 'Well done guys, you got those.' We had to redefine nuisances as positive experiences.

The mantra we had at the time was this: Everybody is in Sales. So if a customer is talking to Ali in customer support, he's the face of the company and he's selling. If a client or prospective client is on to R&D about samples or a new application in the Swedish paper industry, then R&D is selling the company. Anybody who has any kind of interaction with the customer, they're in sales. It was that simple.

My own title changed all the time, depending on what I felt the customer wanted me to be. I had several sets of business cards on the go. If I was talking to a technical person, I was Global Technical Director. I never had a sales card because no one ever wanted to talk to a sales person, so I think the sales one was 'Business Development Manager'. The title never mattered to me, only to the person sitting opposite.

Jayne

Because we were a technical company, because of our historical approach to hiring, BioTector was full of technical people. Our biggest departments were production, calibration and R&D. I don't know if there's an explicit link between being technical and being introverted, but let's just say that our Christmas parties didn't tend to be wild affairs. Mom used always notice that the atmosphere in the canteen tended to be fairly subdued. There was no one saying, 'Hey, did you see Coronation Street last night?'

Jayne was the one person who got through the net. She was the one hire that didn't have to be technical. She was in admin, but as I've said, this doesn't come close to capturing the many roles she filled or the value she contributed. She did a little bit of everything. She worked on financial control with Mom at one stage, she took in orders, she was at every meeting and every interview. She was hugely capable, and as we grew, she became vital to the business.

If you wanted to know what was happening in the company, you went to Jayne. She was the only one who asked how you were, who asked after your kids. She was almost the mother of the whole place. If you thought there was a funny atmosphere in R&D, you could ask her, 'What's going on up there?' Jayne would always know.

You need someone like that, especially when you're travelling a lot.

It wasn't just the office either. She also knew all of our distributors and everything that was going on with them. If there was one characteristic that linked her with everyone else in the company, it was curiosity. For the rest of us, it was a technical curiosity. 'Why did that pump work so well there? Why is that valve better than that valve?' For Jayne, it was the people. She would always be able to uncover the real story behind something. If an order came in from a distributor and a particular box had gone unticked, she'd always be able to say, 'Well, you know what's going on there, you see...'

Everyone loved ringing Jayne and chatting to her.

Factory Acceptance Testing

We had a lot of tests and trials going on, and as these began to bear fruit, and as Hach began to ramp up their efforts, sales began to tick up. At one time, we only sold in ones and twos. Now orders began to come in for five and ten analysers at a time. This was unprecedented. An order for ten units? Amazing! Fantastic! We were thrilled.

Now, instead of spending €40,000 on an order, the client was spending €200,000 or €400,000. Because of the size of the outlay, they would often want to visit the factory and do a factory acceptance test, or FAT for short.

You could have three or four people arriving into the factory to stand in front of the analyser and go through a checklist of questions. We had assumed it would be no more than a box ticking exercise and that the calibration guys would be able to handle it. It would turn out that these FAT visitors were actually quite senior, and that they had a lot of questions about both the unit and the company itself. So who were the best people to come down and talk to them? The R&D guys.

R&D were once again being asked to stop what they were doing and go do things that they found it hard to get excited about. Not alone that, but because these were quite senior people, I felt that I needed to take them out to dinner in the evening.

Everybody's first instinct – including mine – was to regard these FATs as a pain in the ass. I was still travelling all the time, and now these extra duties filled up the weeks I was at home. Frequently too – if they'd travelled from far afield – these trips required quite a bit of entertaining. We'd be finished early and have to take them out to Blarney Castle or down to Cobh. They often turned into week-long events.

But we soon realised that these were actually brilliant opportunities.

We could have regarded the FAT as no more than a compliance event. Here's a list of questions; does the analyser do this? Yes. Does it do that? Yes. We could have left it at that – and most of our competitors did. They handed the visiting party over to a production person with a clipboard, but we saw the opportunity. These people were the Macks and Dons of their companies, the inside influencers who had the potential to become BioTector's strongest advocates. I was flying halfway around the world to meet guys like these. Now, they're actually coming into our factory. There was no airfare. I didn't have to sit on a plane for twenty hours. So this isn't a compliance event, this is a sales event.

We had posters up everywhere detailing our core values and our product leadership strategy. As the customers came in, they could see the culture of the company all around them. They could see what we were attempting to do and what was great about BioTector. They go down to the production floor to do a test and the guy who's doing it knows the analyser inside out. There's no question he can't handle; he can explain why UV persulfate doesn't work, why high temperature doesn't work, why this pump is the optimum pump for this job.

All of our competitors were big companies who just couldn't do this kind of thing. They didn't have innovators in their R&D departments ready to drop everything to go down and walk the client through everything.

As soon as we realised exactly what these FAT trips were, we went all out. I picked them up from the airport, brought them out to the factory. Jayne would be straight out to meet them, then they'd go for a tour. The whole thing was closely choreographed, from start to finish. I'd tell them, 'Piotr from R&D will be with you for the week, he's spent many years developing the analyser, he will be able to answer any questions you have. Ali will be here to look after any training needs'. And I took them out in the night and laid on all of the entertainment.

We got wonderful feedback from these FATs "What an experience. That was amazing. Your people really know what they're talking about."

These clients were buying stuff all around the world, and not just TOC analysers. They told us that they never got the kind of experience, they never encountered the level of engagement they saw in BioTector.

At the beginning, there'd be a general groan when you'd announce an FAT. *Not another one. That's my week gone.* We had to get over that. At the Monday meeting after the FAT, we had this mantra. What did we learn last week? We'd go around the room asking what was learned. So someone would say, "Well, I learned that there's a new project coming up next year", and someone else might say, "I heard that they tried UV persulfate on this other project, and it failed completely."

So we were living our values, promoting that culture of learning, that curiosity. And more importantly, it worked really really well. And everyone knew it did. Ali might come down after an FAT and say, 'Those guys, there's no way they're ever going to order from anyone else. They're BioTector through and through.'

Afterwards if there was someone that they got on particularly well with – be it Piotr or Ali or Philip, they would be deputised to ring the client up and ask how they're getting on. And then six months later, that customer would order ten more analysers. People got a real kick out of it. Ali might say, "They're mine, I sold them." Or Piotr might claim the sale, "That's not your sale, David, R&D made that one."

So we turned these pain-in-the-ass compliance exercises into a huge positive, something that everyone had a stake in, and that reinforced this idea that everyone was a salesperson.

Unity

It was a big cultural shift.

You'd hear arguments going on in corridors. Ok, you don't want too many arguments but sometimes, they're valuable. I remember several times stopping and listening in, and each time, invariably, one of the protagonists would have taken on the role of the customer. Someone would be arguing, 'You can't be doing that, if you do that for every customer, you'll get nothing done'. And someone else would say, 'You have to do it, you can't let the unit out of the factory if you don't...'

I felt that these were good arguments. They suggested that the customer was in our factory all the time, that the customer's needs were always being considered. A lot of this had been with us from the very beginning, but after we settled on a strategy, there were more of these clashes, where the debate would centre on whether or not something was a negative or a positive, a nuisance or an opportunity.

So we had our strategy, we had our focus, we were clear in our own minds who we were. Following on from that, we had clear actions – things like implementing 5S and Lean Manufacturing, like bringing R&D in to support calibration. We had our stores ready so that we had all we needed to ensure we delivered on time. And there was great unity amongst us. We had always thought of ourselves as the underdog and now that we were working with Hach, we saw ourselves as even more of an underdog. We were in with the big boys and would have to fight hard to maintain our identity and to make sure we delivered on the commitments we had made. We instituted daily meetings. At 9:30 every day, seven or eight of us – from R&D, calibration, production, Jayne, Dad (if he was in the office) and me – would get together for a twenty minute catch up and to go through the day's priorities. I saw it as my role to continually bring things back to the strategy, to keep reinforcing the promises we'd made to ourselves. So if there was an FAT coming up, I would say, "Yes, this is frustrating, but here's the benefit..." Or if there were samples coming in that week, I'd ask "Who's doing that?" and point out that this wasn't a distraction, it was an opportunity. I would continually relate what we were doing back to those six values, to make sure we were sticking to them, and that they were at the forefront of everyone's mind. The morning meeting was a brilliant place to tell stories, to repeat what we were about. With success, it's easy to let that kind of thing lapse, to say, everything's going fine, we don't really need this anymore. The reality was that to stay successful, we had to keep getting all of these things right, all the time. We had to stay focused on the reasons why we were where we were, because they were the reasons we would continue to improve.

And we took any opportunity we could to send out other members of staff so they could get a better sense of the bigger picture. If a technical issue popped up in Poland, we would send one of the Polish guys out, and they would come back with stories about how well we were doing there. When we picked up projects in Turkey, Ali flew out to look after them. So staff were getting great experience, they were more plugged into the BioTector story and we were able to deliver solutions without any language barrier. There was huge pride in what they were doing and a bit of a competition element too – how many orders did Turkey get this year and how many orders from Poland?

It was an unwritten rule that we would try to meet twenty customers every month. If I met ten and Dad met five, the last five were usually picked up by R&D or Ali in customer support.

That unity of purpose manifested in unexpected ways. I remember coming in one Monday morning and noticing on the alarm record that calibration had been in over the weekend. I mentioned it in passing to Sabu, our calibration lead, and he said that he had been in on Saturday to complete a test and make sure that an order went out on time. It would turn out that this had been happening quite a bit. Why? During testing, calibration would discover a problem and call on R&D to fix it. R&D would come down, get to work and eventually fix the problem. Great, problem solved, but it had never occurred to me that if the order was to go out on time, this lost time would have to be made up. Calibration recognised this however and without being asked, without making any fuss, they had been staying late or coming in on weekends just to make sure that everything got out on time.

In order to give departments a greater degree of ownership of their work, we instituted monthly meetings where each would present their goals and objectives, and highlight issues that other departments needed to be aware of. Instead of me or Dad asking, "Is that done yet?" the departments took the lead, created their own slides and told us what was happening. This was a complete culture shift. It was very rewarding to see people growing into their roles. They were proud of what they were presenting, and confident in what they said. "This is what we're doing, this is where we are, this is what we need to do to get to the next level." They were effectively benchmarking themselves, setting their own performance indicators.

Take off

If I was doing a lot of travelling before Hach, it went through the roof now. We had to get the whole US and European sales and service teams up and running. While Dad helped a lot, and Ali came on board to do a lot of the service training, most of the travelling fell to me. Taking on sales and service teams in the US and Europe simultaneously was a massive undertaking. All that travel can take its toll on family life, but Sue was always really supportive. "Do what you have to do," she'd say.

I remember we put blue boxes on the calendar around all the days I was going to be away – which was about half the year now. And then, when I got home, there was always an FAT to deal with, so I'd be out at night doing dinners and showing clients around.

I used to say to Sue, "Five years. We'll get this

right in five years..."

We cancelled all of our European distributors. They were all upset, as we knew they would be, but Hach had agreed to offer the best of these the option of coming on as sub-distributors. Within a couple of months, almost all had. A good product is a good product, and distributors, when they have a good product, won't let it go easily. And they understood why we went to Hach, why it was a good move for us.

We got Hach in Europe up and running very quickly, and things took off straight away. Within five months they had hit the 44 sales – the same number we had secured in the whole of the previous year. This was really outstanding. They started from nothing, learned the product then went out and sold it.

The challenge for us was to keep up with them. The production and calibration teams did an amazing job there. Our stores were fully stocked so that there were no log jams there and we were never caught out. No penalty fee was ever paid.

The US was a little slower about getting going. While Hach might have hundreds of salespeople, we identified six or seven who were really good at value selling and who we thought were particularly suited to selling BioTector. These were the ones we needed to spend car time with, explaining the analyser's potential and getting them energised and positive, helping them with those first few sales and allowing that to motivate them. There was a guy in Texas, and a woman in Louisiana who were particularly good. In fact, she won 'Rookie of the year' in Hach for her success selling BioTector.

Overall, that first year was a massive success. We loved what Hach was doing, they loved what we were doing. All of the work was paying off. Sales were going great and everything was really positive.

In 2010, within a year of signing, we sold 106 analysers, almost double the previous year's sales. For the first time, I was getting a bonus for selling more than 90 units. And in the following years, things only got better. In 2013, we sold almost 300 units, a 400% improvement on 2009. It just flew.

The BioTector Team

BioTector Analyser for Wastewater

BioTector System-C
for Clean Water

Myself and Dad
in the workshop

The Hach partnership, a major step to our growth

Product Loss occurring in a Dairy Plant

The first of our awards

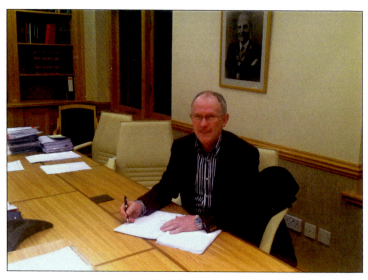

Final Signature on the Acquisition by Danaher

Chapter 6 – Looking East

Things were going so well that in late 2011, Hach suggested we extend our contract to cover China, Japan and South America as well as Europe and the US. We readily agreed. I was doing all the sales training with Jason Padilla, Hach's BioTector product manager. We got on really well; Jason would be my main ally in the company in the years that followed. I also took care of most of the service training. Ali was the expert here, but I could just about manage, and he was at the end of the phone if anything went wrong. And in any case, his documentation, presentations and videos were exceptional, and that made the whole process much easier for everyone.

China

You'd come across a lot of funny little cultural differences. If I was in the US at a sales meeting, it wouldn't be unusual for someone to ask me to service the analyser while I was there. There was an expectation that if you were a BioTector person, you could do that. And that was fine, I *could* do that. But in Asia, it was totally different. If someone mentioned an issue with a unit and I offered to take a look, they'd be scandalised. I was a senior executive; it would be seen as extremely unprofessional for me to pick up a spanner. Instead, they'd find an interpreter and a guy in overalls with a box of tools. *He* would open up the unit and I'd explain through an interpreter, 'You first have to turn that thing over there...'

In America, you always knew exactly where you stood. People are brash and outspoken. I might make a presentation and if anyone took issue with something I said, they would not hold back. A guy might say, "Well, that ain't gonna work", and I'd probe a little further to see what the problem was. And it might turn out that they'd been using a UV persulfate or a high temperature technology, and so I'd explain that BioTector was totally different and didn't have the same flaws. You could thrash things out, "What's your concern here? What's your fear?" In that way, you could arrive at a solution quite quickly.

In Asia, no one would ever say anything vaguely confrontational. No difficult questions, no putting people on the spot. On a sales trip, you could never ask if they were going to order or not. Being direct is the same as being rude.

Before we extended the Hach contract to China, we had a distributor there called Tegent. At my first sales meeting with Tegent and the prospective customer, the only thing the customer wanted to do was talk about me. What's your background? It's a family business? Do you have brothers and sisters? Why didn't your brothers join? How did your father develop the product? After an hour of that, they might broaden it out and ask about the company. And that would be the whole meeting. They didn't want to know a thing about the analyser. I was kind of annoyed at the beginning. I flew all the way out here just to talk about my family? So I went home, waited in hope for an order that didn't come. Instead, I got a call from the distributor. "We need you to come back out again."

"Why? What's the case for going back out? Where are the sales?"

And the distributor would say, "Give it time, give it time. This is how we do it, this is the culture."

So you go back and this time the conversation is a little more technical. Four visits later and there's nothing they don't know about you and your company. They understand your approach, your processes, your company culture, your relationship with your distributors – everything. And they don't want to see a different person on any of these visits, you've got to show up in person, to the point where you've established a close relationship with them. Only then do you get the order.

Much of Asia was like that. Relationship first, then the order. We had to be patient and put in the time, but it did pay off in a tremendous level of loyalty. All of this changed however when we signed with Hach. They were so well known that the endless preliminaries were unnecessary.

I noticed too that in Taiwan and China, you were far more likely to see women working in technical sales roles than you would in the west. In Europe and America, it was only as we started working with Hach and began moving up the value chain in our client companies that we began to deal with women more frequently.

The Sadara Clause

For some time now, we'd been hearing whispers about a Saudi Arabian project called Sadara. There was a real air of mystery about it. Other than the fact that it was a joint venture between Dow Chemicals and Saudi Aramco – the state oil company – there were few firm details. Mack Keeter, our man in Dow, told us that if it went ahead, it would be huge. And if BioTector wanted to be a part of it, we would have to do the groundwork now. Mack warned us that whatever other distributor deals we did, we should take care to ensure that we would be free to deal directly with Sadara, if and when it came to be.

Any orders, he said, might not necessarily come from Saudi Arabia. They might come through China or Holland or the US or wherever. If the project was forced to deal with one distributor in one place and another in another, the chances of us securing a contract would be reduced. They wouldn't want four different prices, four different sets of terms and conditions. The simpler we could make the contract, the better our chances of securing it. For that reason, we were careful to exclude Sadara by name in all distributor contracts that we signed throughout this time, and that includes Hach. We told them the truth, which was that we didn't know if this project was ever going to happen, but if it did, we had been working with Dow for many years, and this would be BioTector's exclusively. It would be our win.

Mack also told us that in order to secure Sadara business, we would need a decent presence in Saudi Arabia. At the time, we had a distributor, but they weren't great, so – after some research – we ended up signing with Dar Al Riyadh. They had a well-established relationship with Saudi Aramco. And of course we made sure that their contract had a Sadara clause too.

Here again is the importance of having a travelling CEO. Because we spent so much time going around learning the market, talking to people, building relationships, we were far more alive to the opportunities. If we hadn't been travelling, if we had just left it to the distributors, they would have had no interest in preparing for an opportunity that might or might not happen three or four years down the line. Their only interest is today's sales, this year's quotas. To put this in context, we were putting the Sadara clause into our contracts in 2010, but didn't actually get a single order until 2013.

The language barrier

I remember being at quite a few Chamber of Commerce and Enterprise Ireland talks, where the issue under discussion was international growth, and getting into non-English speaking countries in particular. The thing that always came up in these sessions was the fact that we're not great at languages in this country.

This was never an issue for us. I often stood up at these events and said that we were in 52 countries despite the fact that we only spoke English. And bear in mind that BioTector is a niche product which requires a lot of in-depth explanation. There's no doubt that it would have been useful to have a multi-lingual team on the ground but in truth language was never a barrier. We could always find a way around it. If a distributor aspires to attract the best international products, they will have to have English. We always found too that if there is more than one language around the table, everyone tends to move to English. In the Middle East in general, and in Saudi Arabia in particular, English is the default choice. In short, language was never a reason not to go somewhere. There was always a workaround. I mentioned earlier that we had a great distributor in Korea who had very poor English, and yet he still sold quite a few analysers at key times for us.

It would be different of course if you were setting up an office over there and you wanted to put in a sales or a service team. We were lucky in that regard because we always went in through a third party, and that third party generally had good English.

I think too a lot of Irish start-ups and SMEs have a fear of going too far from home. Irish companies don't target the Middle East or the Far East half as much as we perhaps should. We went on a trade mission to Saudi with Enterprise Ireland and Simon Coveney, who was the Irish Minister for Agriculture at the time. These missions were always really useful because they drew in a range of potential clients that would be really hard to access otherwise. I was interviewed by RTE at the time, and the interviewer was very negative about being there at all. He talked about how difficult it was to break into Saudi; the paperwork, the regulations, the long wait for a visa and so on. Why, he wanted to know, would you bother at all?

I always found Saudi a great country in which to do business. There's a great deal of caution among prospective customers out there simply because so many have been burned by sellers who fail to support their product afterwards. Yes, there is hassle involved in dealing with Saudi. There's a lot of paperwork, and you have to send your passport to Dublin once every three months to get it stamped if you want to keep visiting, but if you prove that you're in it for the long haul – as in Asia – you are repaid with fantastic loyalty.

At the height of my travels, I had two passports on the go. One for business trips to Europe, the US and Israel and one for business trips to the rest of the world. At the time, getting into Saudi was difficult if you had been to Israel, and in any case, it took ten days for the Saudi Embassy to stamp the passport and get it back to you, so if you were flying in the meantime, you needed a backup.

So many stamps tended to draw a lot of attention when we went on holidays, particularly when we were trying to get into the States. I would explain that I travelled for my company, so they would naturally ask which company. The fact that it had 'Bio' in the name tended to prompt a double take, and another twenty questions.

Jayne was a key figure when it came to breaking into any new market. I'd just tell her we had a new distributor in Timbuktu, and ask her to find out what we would have to do to ship there. She'd come back with a detailed list. These lists were long, and they did generate a lot of tedious work, but that was all that stood between us and a brand new, potentially highly lucrative market. Why wouldn't we invest the time and energy in it? Which isn't to say there were no problems. Stuff sometimes got stuck in customs because we hadn't filled out some form, but we figured it out as we went along and never made the same mistake twice.

Around 50% of our workforce was non-national. This wasn't by design; that's just how it worked out, but it did give us an international flavour, and it meant we had no fear of different languages or cultures. Each time I was due to fly out to somewhere new, I'd look over the Wikipedia entry about how to behave, what to say, what not to say and so on. And again, I have to say that Enterprise Ireland is a fantastic organisation when it comes to helping you to navigate new markets.

Kill Astro

By late 2011, the details of the mystical Sadara project finally emerged. It was definitely going ahead and it would need 100 TOC analysers. Half were for process wastewater applications. The other fifty were clean water applications. We saw detailed drawings, showing where the analysers were to go and what they needed to measure.

Thanks to our new Saudi distributor, we had made sales to Saudi Aramco and established good relationships there. They had also come to Ireland for an FAT earlier in the year. Saudi FATs tended to involve more entertainment and last a little longer than conventional FATs. In any case, because of those sales to Saudi Aramco, we had a 9 Com number. This was Aramco's stamp of approval. It indicated that they had tested your products, were happy with them and that you were an approved vendor. On top of that, it turned out that BioTector also had an advocate in an influential position inside Saudi Aramco. His name was Vedula Suryanarayana. He had come across – and been impressed by – the analyser some years before through a relationship with our Dutch distributor. The other thing in our favour was the fact that Mack Keeter was the lead on the Dow Chemicals side. It was to be his last big assignment before retirement. He and Mr. Suryanarayana were to oversee the selection of all analysers on the project.

So that was all great. The one fly in the ointment was that while we might have been very well positioned for the wastewater applications, it was clear that we were not in line for the clean water ones.

A little detail is necessary here. If you want to heat up a process, one of the standard methods is to pump steam through a pipe that runs alongside your process pipe. Conversely, if you want to cool a process, you draw in river water and run that alongside the process pipe. The risk is that the process pipe develops a pinhole leak and leaches contaminants into its neighbour. This is where the clean water analyser comes in. You place it on the cooling or condensate pipe in order to detect the first traces of contaminant, before they wreck the boiler in the case of the condensate pipe, or get into the water course in the case of the cooling pipe.

We had a few analysers deployed in positions like these around the world, and we could see from the way in which the market was evolving that these condensate and cooling water applications were becoming more important.

The difficulty for us however was that BioTector's unique ability to tolerate dirty materials didn't count for much here. The customer would justifiably say, "I don't really need a BioTector here. I can use something that's half the price."

That's where our old Nemesis, the Astro came in. It *was* half the price, and it did well – or at least it did ok – in these clean water applications. And because Hach was so good at selling, it was installed in a very large number of these situations around the world.

Since I mention the Astro. We had one line in our 2010 strategy; well, not really one line. Two words. *Kill Astro.* We wanted Hach to ditch this product, the one that had done so much damage to the reputation of TOC analysers everywhere. We wanted to be so successful that one fine day, Hach would say, "Right that's it, we don't need Astro anymore. Let's stick with BioTector." Throughout our dealings with Hach, even as things got better and better, that little goal was there at the back of our minds the whole time. *Kill Astro.*

System C

Anyway, Mack was very clear about what we could and couldn't get out of Sadara. He more or less said that while BioTector was looking good for the dirty water applications, we were not going to be specified for the clean water ones. They would most likely come from either Shimadzu, a Japanese company, or Starr, a Texan company.

So we asked ourselves the question. Could we build an analyser more appropriate to this application? A simpler, cheaper one, which used the same analysis technology but wouldn't need the features necessary to tolerate dirty process materials. Because it was the necessity of handling dirty water, together with the corrosive nature of the chemical reaction, that made BioTector so expensive in the first place. We couldn't use stainless steel because stainless steel would be eaten up in a matter of months. Instead we used Hastelloy – a nickel based super alloy developed to withstand corrosion in severe environments. All of our components were specified so that they wouldn't be devoured by either the chemistry or the material BioTector had to process. That resilience comes at a price.

Dad, Marek and Seamus got cracking. Marek prepared a detailed set of 3D drawings and Dad met Mack in the UK to discuss project requirements. Effectively, he began selling him something that we didn't actually have. Mack said, "Look, you've got a very small window here, but I trust you guys. Get me a prototype. Fast."

This was 2011. Now, on top of all of R&D's new sales-enabling responsibilities, they also had to tackle this massive project, and with a faster turnaround time than anything we'd attempted before. And yet this was how we always behaved. Myself or Dad would be on a sales call and the customer would start talking about a problem in the process. The sample was too hot and needed to be cooled down, or there was sand in the sample that needed to be taken out. We'd always say "We can sort that out. We can give you a price for solving that." So we'd come back to R&D, give them a drawing and say, "We need that. Can you build it?"

This was always Dad's approach. Don't build it and take it to market. Sell it first, then build it. There was never really any money-making intention in these little additions and modifications. They simply enabled sales, and differentiated us from our competitors, who simply didn't have the flexibility to react to opportunities as we did.

The new analyser needed to be small. Space tended to be tight in these condensate and cooling water applications, so in place of our large unit, we needed a slim analyser one third of the size. Electronics, screen, everything had to fit into one box. We also had to reduce the cost very substantially. Mack had looked for a €10,000 price point, but we decided that this was unrealistic. The customer will always overreach when it comes to price. We were pretty sure that if we could deliver the product as specified, Mack would tolerate a higher price, so we aimed for a 40% discount, reducing the price from €40,000 to around €25,000.

The initial reaction in R&D was negative. "We can't do that. Not a hope. Never going to happen."

"Well," said Dad, "that's what you need to do."

This was one of those projects where constraint fuels innovation. This was thinking inside the box. Here are the limitations – it can't be bigger than this and it can't cost more than this. Go build it. It's the narrow focus that releases the creativity. That's the theory anyway.

So R&D went away, worked at it and came back with a breakthrough. "Look at this! We can do it," they said, "but the box needs to be a small bit bigger."

Dad shook his head. "No, the box can't be any bigger. Sorry. Try again."

This happened several times. Marek and Piotr, under Seamus' supervision, kept at it, kept asking questions about how the analyser was put together, kept testing assumptions, kept trying new things, installing new materials and new components. Do we really need hastelloy *here*? Does the pump need to be this big? With each step closer to the solution, we actually discovered things that allowed us to improve the original BioTector unit. One of these – a mixer reactor – we actually ended up patenting. Valves were changed, pumps were changed, motors were changed and we delivered Mack's prototype, exactly as he had specified just in time, by the skin of our teeth.

The result? Sadara was all BioTector, all one hundred applications. A combination of Mack's faith and the craft and determination of the R&D team stole a 50 analyser order from the competition. And because of the Sadara clause that we had been putting in all new distributor contracts for the preceding three years, all of that revenue was ours, which meant that effectively, the 100 analyser sale was as good as selling 200 analysers.

Chapter 7 – The Product Loss Breakthrough

I mentioned in chapter three that Ohmart VEGA had commissioned an animated video to help explain how the analyser worked. Well, Seamus O'Mahony's son Billy used to come in during the summers for work experience. It turned out that he was particularly skilled in this type of thing and was able to create a range of animated videos which we used for everything from sales to service training. He created an especially brilliant one for System C.

There was a risk inherent in developing this new product of course. The last thing we wanted was for the new analyser to cannibalise the market for the old one. The fear was that the sales guys would see this cheaper product as interchangeable and sell it into applications where it couldn't survive, thereby ruining our hard-won reputation. So we had to be very clear on exactly where it could and couldn't go.

Through the second half of 2011, we made several more hires and the office began to fill up. Dad decided at this point that it was time to get out of the office we shared.

He moved upstairs, a little further away from the centre of things, but close enough to answer questions and discuss ideas. While our roles hadn't changed on paper, I'd become more of an MD, and he more like a chairman or a consultant.

Up to this point, I hadn't needed to be involved in the day-to-day financial operation of the company because Mom, in her financial controller role, oversaw everything so well. She handled wages, bank accounts, money management and tax returns. She also worked very closely with our outside accountant, Adrian Galvin, to prepare accounts for the end of year audit. At this point, however, she decided that if the company was to grow as projected, we would need an additional full time accountant, preferably someone with the capacity to take on the role of financial controller at a future date.

New Hires

We needed an accountant who could look into the numbers and be able to make a story out of them, someone who could call up distributors, for example, and say, "You've got this many analysers, so you should be ordering this number of service kits. You're not. Why? Are you buying non-BioTector parts?"

We needed information to explore new revenue paths. Why are analysers being sold at full price here, but are deeply discounted there? Why are so many optional extras being sold in this market, but none in this?

These were the kinds of stories hidden in the numbers that Mom, with all her other responsibilities, didn't have the time to tease out.

We discovered quite by accident that the South Korean distributor was quoting exorbitant prices for the analyser. It turned out that this was because two years free servicing was a standard feature of contracts over there. Invariably, he'd get bargained down, but the free servicing depleted his revenue stream, so in response, he began sourcing service parts from our suppliers rather than us. We warned him that we couldn't stand over parts that didn't come through us. "They might look the same," we pointed out, "but they mightn't perform the same." There were sites in Germany where they decided that they didn't like the circulation pump in the analyser. They would take it out and install the one they preferred. This of course caused unforeseen problems down the line, and it took time and energy to solve them. There were all sorts of idiosyncrasies like these among the various markets and distributors, and they always left a trail in the numbers.

We needed someone who could follow that trail and pick up these anomalies so that we could do something about them.

Up to now, when we'd needed to hire key people, the vast majority had been technical, and both Dad and Seamus were on firm ground and knew exactly what they wanted. You could tell the first day if the new person knew what they were talking about. But hiring an accountant when you don't have any of those skills yourself is a different prospect. We also needed to hire someone into a senior sales role. Dad was reducing his travelling, and I was more or less maxed out on mine. So this was two senior people we needed to get into the management team as quickly as we could. They needed to be what Jim Collins would call 'A' type people. Self-motivated, good communicators, good leaders. I've always felt that interviews are a flawed means of hiring someone into an organization. No matter what science you put behind it, you just don't know who you're getting.

We hired a sales person first. An unexpected benefit of the fact that Dad was gone from the desk alongside mine was that I could install the new person in my office. It was uncomfortable for both of us, but it allowed me to find out very quickly if they were going to work. And if they were the right person, they would be perfectly positioned in my office to learn everything they needed to learn.

Again I come back to this core quality shared by everyone in the company. Curiosity. Are they curious? Are they absorbing what's going on around them? People were in and out to me all day, so there were great opportunities to learn what we were doing. The right person would be full of questions.

It turned out that this sales guy had no real interest, so we let him go. Then Mom hired an accountant and we did the same thing. Put him in my office to see what would happen. Same problem. He had no real interest in how the company worked, he had no questions to ask. The next person – Margaret Fuentes – was interviewed on the basis of a recommendation Mom had from a colleague in the insurance industry. We knew from day one that Margaret was perfect for the job. She was genuinely interested in everything that was happening and was able to get up to speed very quickly, to the point, in fact, that she was able to take on the financial controller role, leaving Mom free to concentrate on her directorial role.

In order to do the job we needed her to do, she had to get to know each distributor really well, she had to know what countries they were in, what customers they had, which sector and so on. Margaret was just brilliant. She got it, right from the beginning. In the meantime, we decided to put the sales role on ice and get on with other things.

New Applications

Now too we began to bring more rigour to selling BioTector in non end-of-pipe applications. We didn't have figures which would demonstrate the value of deploying TOC analysis earlier in the process but we were trialling different applications and learning a lot from our customers.

We began to structure an argument around product loss prevention. Suppose you're processing oil, and you install an analyser *here*, at a drain in your factory. Then something goes wrong. Oil escapes from something, leaks into the drain, the analyser picks it up and triggers an alarm. Then you go and find the broken valve, the stalled pump, the burst pipe, whatever it is. That way, you don't lose half as much oil as you would if you were waiting for a maintenance schedule or visual inspection to pick it up. And of course it's not just oil. Go into a dairy plant or a brewery and there are pipes running everywhere. All it takes is an operator error or a mechanical breakdown and hundreds if not thousands of Euros worth of valuable process material is lost.

Human behaviour – we would discover – was a big risk factor in dairy. A guy is coming to the end of his shift and a tank isn't emptying fast enough. So he just sluices it down the drain. If we were to monitor the drain, wouldn't that close off that risk and save the company money?

We knew that there were other stories like this out there, and that we could use them to build a case for buying BioTector on cost saving grounds. The trick would be to go from 'You may be losing product' to 'BioTector can save you X Euros'.

Some customers had already figured this out and were using BioTector in process control applications. Mars, for example bought a BioTector from Hach, and word got back to us that the analyser had paid for itself in three days. Three days! There had been a major malfunction in the factory, the analyser had picked it up, an alarm had gone off and a team was dispatched to fix the fault. If it had been missed, €70,000 worth of product would have been lost.

Sometimes a distributor would drop us a line. 'Big malfunction caught by BioTector. Well done lads. Saved the company a fortune.'

What's a fortune? That was the big question.

Andrew McDonald of EASL was one of the people that helped us answer it. He was one of a number of distributors that we retained in Ireland. If you remember, we kept Ireland out of the Hach arrangement. We had customers and reference sites here that we wanted to remain close to, and we also had several distributors.

Andrew was a phenomenal solution seller. His focus was dairy. At the time, the team was very busy getting the Hach sales and service guys online, so Dad worked with Andrew to try to tease out what was going on in dairy, to work out how we could help them and how we might begin to build financials into the sales argument.

Andrew's genius move was to actually buy a Transit van and deck it out with a BioTector and a big screen. He would drive to customer car parks, open up the van and give presentations inside. Afterwards, he would ask if he could back the van up to the plant and let the intake pipe down into a drain, just to see if much product was being lost. He even had a vacuum sampler if he couldn't get the van in close enough. He'd leave the analyser hooked up overnight, then the following day, he'd come back and show the client all of the spikes in the chart, indicating periods when milk leaking into the drain drove the TOC content through the roof.

These spikes corresponded with a variety of adverse events. For example, if the tanker driver was under pressure for time, or was careless, milk would end up running into the drain. Sometimes, the cause would be a leaking pipe. Because there are so many miles of pipework in these plants, a lot of milk can disappear before anyone knows anything about it. In another scenario, an operator might have to move product from one tank to another. Again, if they're careless, or if a faulty level sensor tells them that a tank is empty when it's not, product gets lost. It's usually a case of tell nobody, clean it up and get on with things.

We now had to understand product processing on a much deeper level than we ever did before. I'd talk to waste treatment plant managers and ask them when and where they saw spikes and what they might be related to. I remember in one dairy, the guy told me that every Tuesday, without fail, he'd see huge TOC spikes.

"Do you know why?" I asked him.

He rolled his eyes. "The Tuesday night shift up in the yoghurt plant. They're useless, they're always throwing stuff down the drain."

As far as he was concerned, this was just a headache he had to deal with. The actual value of the lost product never occurred to him. But he was in the perfect position to tell us where the problems were. Our job was to take that insight to the process people and say, "Do you realise how much stuff you're losing? Why not trial an analyser? Put it *here* and you'll see exactly what's going down the drain."

We ran into quite a bit of denial at this point. The process guys would tell us that there was no problem with the process, that losses – if there were any at all – were miniscule.

This is where Andrew's BioTector Transit van came in. He would say to the client, "I'll give you the van for the week. Stick the intake in the drain and leave it there. What have you got to lose?"

Several times, the product losses so shocked the client that they would refuse to give him his van back and he had to call Dad to get a lift home. We would have to deliver a new analyser in record time just so Andrew could get back on the road.

Marketing

We always had a very strong learning culture in BioTector. Myself and the other members of the management team did quite a few courses, and we managed to take something away from almost every one. And we were always quick to make changes based on what we had learned.

Myself, Ian and our new financial controller Margaret went on a course called Management4Growth. It was run over ten weeks by DIT with support from Enterprise Ireland. Each week you focused on a different section of your business and in the end you created a montage of what had been implemented as a result of what you had learned. So someone would give a presentation on a particular topic, then you'd break up into groups and talk about that issue. While the participants mightn't be in the same sector as you, they were all around the same size, and there tends to be a lot of common ground. You'd find out things in those chats and on coffee breaks that could end up being very useful.

At the same time, we began a marketing audit with Enterprise Ireland called Strategic Marketing Review, or SMR for short. Our experience with this and Management4Growth showed us that we didn't actually know what marketing was. We had thought of it as a fancy brochure or a slick website, but of course that wasn't it at all.

We had actually hired a marketing person at one point. She had a great CV, and probably would have excelled in the marketing department of a big firm, but because we couldn't tell her what to do, she ended up sliding into an admin role. This was a waste of her talents, but we couldn't direct her because we didn't know how. Our failing here, combined with what we were learning in the SMR lead us to the conclusion that we actually needed to outsource marketing to an expert.

Enterprise Ireland recommended Mel Galloway. She was available part time, so we took her on as a marketing consultant two to three days per week. She turned out to be brilliant. We explained that we needed to build a story around product loss prevention and she understood exactly what was needed. She began a series of interviews – with me, with Dad, with Jayne, with Seamus, with Andrew, with a range of our customers. She was a wonderful communicator, very skilled at finding out what she needed to know, very skilled at recruiting people to help her.

Her initial focus was on dairy industry losses. She said to R&D, 'Ok, I know when you sample the stuff going down the drain, you're measuring total organic carbon, but is there any way of converting that to litres of milk?'

Ali set out to answer that question. We bought all kinds of milk – low fat, full fat, semi-skimmed, milk fortified with vitamins – Milk is among the nastiest stuff you can put through an analyser. Any residue is going to smell vile after a couple of days, but of course because our chemical reaction is so aggressive, there was no residue – the analyser self-cleans as it goes.

This of course was more sales-enabling work from R&D, but by now they were on message and could see the value in what they were doing. And in any case, Ali loved the project and threw himself into it. Eventually, he was able to work out a conversion factor for full fat milk. When we combined that with a flow rate, we could amend the software so that in addition to TOC, we got a reading for milk lost. Armed with this information, we were able to arrive at some pretty shocking conclusions. Most dairies were losing between 3% and 5% of everything they bought. This was huge. What's more, these losses were going down drains and ending up in the waste treatment plant, and that meant that not alone was product being lost, additional resources were needed to treat this waste. One local dairy client allowed Mel full access to their processes and figures, and while they didn't give us permission to use these figures in our promotional materials, we were able to extrapolate from those figures to create a calculator which we could then use to demonstrate the losses issue to other dairies.

We were able to work out that if a typical dairy cut their losses by just 15%, they would save themselves €600,000 per year. Factor in the reduction in treatment costs as a result of that saving and that figure grew by €105,000 to €705,000. Again, that's based on a 15% reduction in losses. Typically, we found that after BioTector was installed, dairies saved themselves anywhere between 25% and 40%. Glanbia told us that some of the plants in which they'd installed BioTector had reduced waste product discharged by 40%, which corresponded with a payback period of just three months. This was way faster than we had anticipated. Not only that, there was also a big reduction in the loading to the treatment plant, and the elimination of an odour problem that had dogged them for years.

Carberry Group had already bought analysers from Andrew, thanks to his work with the BioTector van. Mel followed up with them and found out that their yield had gone up, while energy costs in the waste water treatment plant had fallen significantly. In fact, they reported that the environmental and commercial value of the first analyser they bought justified the purchase of ten more within eight months. Before this, there was no real way of knowing where waste was occurring during processing. A typical dairy could process over 1.3 million litres of milk each day. It came into the box, it went out of the box and 5% was gone. Where? Nobody could say. Now, they could zero in on process vulnerabilities and take remedial action. BioTector became the key to unlocking huge chunks of value. If they were losing 70,000 litres per day – which would not be unusual – they could ask, 'What do we need to do to reduce that by 20%?' Do we need more maintenance? Do we need to tighten nuts? Replace old motors? Increase visual inspections? Check level sensors? Many of the improvements prompted by BioTector revelations came down to human behaviour. Simply telling operators and truck drivers that we were now monitoring drains was enough to prompt a massive reduction in milk flowing down those drains.

In Carberry, they connected the analyser to an alarm system. If the analyser detected product where product should not be, there were flashing lights and sirens. In another dairy, they set up an auto-text system. Everybody knew that when the message came in, you dropped everything and ran. Process people began to understand their plants a little better. They saw where the issues were and addressed them, by changing components or implementing new maintenance procedures. Huge savings were made.

None of this work would have been possible without Mel. She was able to ask the right questions and knew exactly what to do with the answers. And she forged such great relationships with the clients that two of them were prepared to allow us to use this information in our marketing materials, while the third gave us open access to their numbers and processes.

Now we needed to take these lessons further afield.

Awards

Throughout this phase, Hach continued to drive sales higher and higher. In every new territory, the speed with which they achieved sales was something to behold. Their sales processes were exceptional, their sales people were exceptional and we could only look on in admiration as the orders came flooding in.

Their service processes were a little slower to come up to speed. This was largely due to the fact that they had specialised in the US municipal sector up to this point. There, attitudes to servicing are a little more casual. If a unit breaks down on Tuesday, it's ok to pop in on Thursday or Friday to fix it. In industry, it's got to be fixed now. No excuses. With Ali's help however they ramped up their efforts very quickly and within a matter of months servicing was every bit as good as sales.

In March of 2012, we won AIB's Manufacturer of the Year award, and on the night, we also took home the Chairman's Award. We were thrilled. It was the first time we'd entered anything like this, and while there was quite a bit of work for myself and Mel in preparing the entry, winning gave everyone a great boost. It was particularly gratifying that this was a manufacturing award given all the work production had done over the previous two years.

Soon after that, we won a Frost and Sullivan product leadership award. To give it its full title, it was the 2012 United States Water and Wastewater Analytical Instrumentation Product Leadership Award. It may not sound like much, but it was actually really significant. Frost and Sullivan benchmarked us and our competitors across a range of weighted criteria, including product quality and acceptance in the marketplace, giving us a final score of 9 out of 10. Our nearest competitor scored 6.6. This is from the report: 'Penetrating the Water and Wastewater Analytical Instrumentation market with new and unknown technologies poses a daunting challenge for players in this market space. (BioTector) penetrated the market successfully by employing its technology in traditionally difficult applications around the United States, like in the Oil Refining and Petrochemical industry in Texas, for example. Through Best Practices and a compelling word-of-mouth reputation BioTector Analytical Systems successfully developed robust organic growth across the U.S.'

Not only that but it was able to put a figure on market share. 'BioTector Analytical Systems is constantly seeking new avenues for its acclaimed products. As part of the company's continued effort to gain market share, BioTector constantly develops add-on value services and it extends its product line to accommodate ever evolving needs in the marketplace. This product and market development strategy has enabled BioTector Analytical Systems to become a market leader with an estimated 25–30 percent share of the TOC Water and Wastewater Analytical Instrumentation market. BioTector is a highly effective role model for product leadership.'

Now, for the first time, we had an accurate picture of position in the market. The news that we had somewhere between a 25% and 30% share in the US was a source of great delight. We were a small Irish company who had developed, from scratch, a technology that became the market leader in the US. How many companies can say that? And the fact that it was product leadership made it particularly special. This was an endorsement of the product leadership strategy we had committed to two years earlier. Here too was formal recognition that we had met our original goal – to build the best analyser in the world.

One other thing worth mentioning at this point. In the first chapter, I listed the fact that ours was a non-standard technology as one of the major barriers to entry we faced. Dr. Ali Demir – to give him his full title – had, in the meantime, produced a series of white papers on the BioTector oxidation process and through this work succeeded in having that process formally approved as a standard method of TOC analysis.

Very soon after the Frost and Sullivan award, we won both an exporters and distributors award and an innovation award. It was as if every part of our business was being celebrated in each of these wins. We made a big deal of all of these and made sure to let everyone know that these were awards that they had earned.

Hach played a central role in all of this. Their success was intertwined with ours. If they hadn't been so successful in driving sales, we would not have been producing sufficient numbers to enable the manufacturing award, let alone the product leadership one.

Robert

Two further things emerged from that Management4Growth programme I mentioned. One was my formal adoption of the CEO title. I already held this role effectively, but changing the business card made sense from the point of view of distributors and customers.

We also realised that we had to move on hiring the other sales person. During one of those exercises on the course, they asked us which market we most wanted to increase sales in. All three of us – Margaret, Ian and I – agreed that the answer to this was Saudi Arabia. Next, they asked us to list all of the people – business contacts, politicians, whoever – that might be able to help. It was then that the name 'Robert Stevens' popped into my head.

He worked for one of the first distributors we had in Europe. They were not a particularly good distributor *for us* – we cancelled them quite early on – but Robert had stood out as a star performer. I bumped into him in an airport at one stage and I remembered him telling me how much he was doing in the Middle East. When I got back to the office, I gave him a call, then met him the following week at an exhibition we both happened to be attending.

The following month he was on the payroll.

Robert had a dual role. First of all, we wanted him to take on the Middle East. Second of all we wanted him to help out with Hach Lange in Europe. They were doing great, but we felt – given all we'd learned – that they could do even better, plus we also wanted to keep a close eye on what they were doing. Robert spoke Dutch and German, and he lived right on the German border in Holland, so he was perfectly placed. And they loved him in Hach Lange. He was a brilliant solution seller and knew the technology really well, so he facilitated dozens of sales. He clocked up huge numbers of miles flitting around Europe, but he loved it, and it was all really worthwhile. A German company – LAR – had a stranglehold on the German market but within a year, Robert had made significant inroads. Germany was a very important market because it has a significant influence on China. If a product does well in Germany, it invariably takes off there.

It was around this time that the trouble started.

Chapter 8 – The Struggle to Stay Independent

Any small company working with a big company will have all kinds of fears. Many of ours were justified, but one in particular was not. The fear that they would come in and somehow exploit our technology? That turned out to be completely groundless. Danaher, Hach's owner, is a very large organisation with a jealously guarded reputation. They could not be seen to be abusing their power. And they were an acquisitions company. If they acquired a reputation for being predatory, no one would talk to them. Once the contract was signed, Hach actually began coaching us on maintaining the integrity of our IP. They told us to mark documents 'confidential', to put disclaimers in emails, to only share documents with them that absolutely needed to be shared.

Uncertainty

But the fear that we would become wholly dependent on Hach or tied up with them in some way? That was real.

Not long after we had signed, we got a visit from Hach senior management. It was very clear to us that this visit was all about finding ways of drawing us more deeply into their organisation. Just as at the original negotiation, they zeroed in on R&D and suggested that we co-operate on product development. Determined to maintain our independence, we very politely declined. Not long after that, Dad got a call out of the blue from a former Hach employee, who said, "You did the right thing side-stepping that R&D co-operation stuff. I love the fact that you're a family business and you're keeping that culture going. Just be careful in the future."

That warning chimed with our own suspicions. The difficulty was that the more successful the relationship became, the more difficult it was to retain that independence. Throughout the early years of the contract – 2010 and 2011 – when things were only getting better and better, that nagging doubt, those fears were easy to ignore. But as 2012 wore on, they began to resurface again.

New Strategy

By mid 2012, Hach made up 77% of our sales. This was great of course, but we couldn't help but be troubled by our growing level of dependence on them. I mentioned these concerns to the other participants on that Enterprise Ireland programme I talked about in the last chapter. I told them how well things were going and how sales had increased and so on, but that I feared for our independence. Hach was well known to quite a few of the other participants, and they all thought I was worried over nothing. "They're an amazing company, what are you worried about? Give them the whole world and double your sales."

I wasn't reassured. So, in mid-2012, the management team sat down and re-evaluated our 2010 strategy. This team was now much stronger, much more well-rounded, and included Mel, Robert Stevens and our financial controller, Margaret. Dad was also back in the room so that we could tap into his experience.

We agreed that while things had gone according to plan, we needed to make some changes. We had the right people in the right positions doing the right things. In 2010 we wanted to sell loads of analysers, and we still wanted to do that in 2012. But now, in addition, we agreed that we would aim to reduce our dependence on Hach, to reduce their proportion of our sales from 77% to 50%. Not by reducing Hach's sales, but by increasing non-Hach sales. And the Middle East was central to that strategy.

Terry, who had been heavily involved in the original contract negotiation, was in charge of the TOC business unit in Hach – he was basically my opposite number there. We worked closely together, organising training and enabling sales and so on. In the lead up to this phase, all of our meetings with Hach were really positive; everyone telling everyone else how great they were, high fives all round and so on. 2010 was a fantastic year, 2011 was better, 2012 was already looking like it was going to blow the other two out of the water.

But Robert's arrival prompted some head scratching in the US. Terry wanted to know why we'd hired him. Robert was a German speaker based in Holland, but Hach Lange was our distributor there; we couldn't make sales ourselves. Despite the fact that Hach Lange was delighted with how Robert was enabling sales, Terry remained dubious.

We'd signed Hach up for Europe, America, Japan, China and South America. They set their sights on the Middle East at about the same time that we did. Now, for the first time, we were dragging our feet, we weren't jumping at the opportunity to add a new market to the Hach contract. We were cajoled and coaxed, and while we were always unfailingly polite, we resisted. This is how Hach twigged that our new strategy differed from the old one.

The converse of our growing dependence on Hach

was of course their growing dependence on us. BioTector had become the market leader in the US. It was rapidly becoming a very successful product for Hach, and yet they had very little control over us, which made us a risk, and that was a headache for Terry, whose job it was to manage that risk. They saw us hiring people like Robert and knew that we could do this because of their brilliance at selling. From a Hach point of view, Robert was learning a great deal from his close contact with Hach Lange and was going off to the Middle East to put all he had learned into practice.

System C

Things got worse when they refused to take on our new condensate and cooling water analyser, System C.

"You're our route to market," we said, "you can't refuse to take it."

Terry told us that Hach was under no obligation to take on every new thing we developed. "We'll sell the one we agreed to sell, but we decide what we bring to market. We are partners but we're also competitors," we were told. "And this product you've developed is in direct competition with our Astro."

I remember hanging up the phone and thinking,

did he just call us competitors? Up to this point, we'd only ever referred to each other as partners. Any positioning, any strategising – that all happened under the surface, it was never acknowledged. We'd only ever been positive about each other to each other. Now for the first time we were being given a clear signal that things had changed, that our resistance to signing the Middle East had consequences.

And I could see things from Terry's point of view. Suppose he did take on System C in all of their territories. It was, as he said, in direct competition with Astro. But he couldn't sell System C in the Middle East because we already had a different distributor there. Instead he sells the Astro. But now his customers there will say, "Hang on, you're selling System C in the US, but you're trying to push the Astro here instead?" There would be an undeniable credibility issue.

We checked the contract and confirmed that Hach were not obliged to take it on. So that was that. We were locked out of the US, Europe, Japan, China and South America.

We decided not to make a big deal out of it, but nor did we give up. We went ahead and launched System C globally ourselves. And every time we had a conversation with a Hach person – in sales, in service, whatever – we brought up System C and told them all about it.

Very many of these people shared our views of the Astro and couldn't understand why they weren't being given access to a better product. So now numerous sales guys in Hach started getting onto Terry and giving him hassle about it.

This irritated Terry even more. He told us, "You've got to stop talking about this thing. We're not taking it, and I'm sick of my sales guys getting on to me about it."

But of course we never stopped talking about it. Any time we were on the road – sharing the car with a sales guy – we'd say, "Did you hear about System C?"

"Yeah, I heard about it, what's the price point?"

And we'd give them all the details. Invariably, they'd start asking awkward questions. "This is great, why can't we sell this?"

Terry threw us a bone and said look, we'll do a 'voice of the customer' survey, which was a questionnaire they send out to customers. Lo and behold that came back two weeks later and we were told, "Results were negative, this is not what the customer wants at all."

But of course you'll never get a useful answer from a survey like that. Henry Ford famously said that if he asked people what they wanted, they would have said faster horses. And there's no way we'd ever have built BioTector if we'd based our plans on market survey data. Customers will always focus on either speed of measurement, price or both. Our view was that the survey was designed to return a negative result, to give credibility to the refusal to list System C.

"You don't understand the market," we were told. "We're Hach, we're experts and we're just not going to take it on."

We pushed back as much as we felt we could, then went ahead and pushed System C everywhere else. The product sat in a niche within a niche, but it actually went very well and we got great feedback from customers and distributors. We made very sure that all of this got back to Terry.

From there however, our relationship only became more complicated. If we had just given them the world – and they found it hard to see why we wouldn't – everything would have been easy, but we didn't, so it wasn't, and really, it was both of our faults.

Enterprise Ireland had a programme where you could take on a graduate out of the Smurfit School of Business in UCD and EI would pay most of their salary for the year. Joanna joined the company under this programme. She was great – really sharp, really capable. The plan was that she would get up to speed on all we were doing with dairy, then travel out to the US and help Hach to crack that market. We'd discussed this with Hach at an earlier stage and they were very enthusiastic. Not anymore. We were told that we were competitors and that Joanna would not be going over.

Down Under

Again, this was bad news, but we thought about it and said, "Ok, fine. We'll send her to Australia and New Zealand. Loads of dairy applications over there." We sounded Joanna out on this and she was happy with the change of plans, so we gave her all the training and she travelled around with Andrew for a bit before flying out to Australia. She worked with our existing distributor – a company called Pryde – and effectively did what Andrew had been doing in Ireland. We sent out an analyser on a little trolley so that she could bring it around on the back of a pickup. She would wheel it into dairies just as Andrew had done here. And all of the information she gathered came back to Mel here in Cork, and Mel would continue to build these wonderful stories around it, all of which demonstrated tremendous returns on investment.

In one dairy in South Australia, the process guy told Joanna that he knew he was losing product, so she set up the analyser to monitor the drains for a week. When she came back, there were way fewer losses than expected. The following week, after she took the analyser away, the process guy was sure he was losing substantial amounts of milk again, so he called Joanna back...And again, the losses disappeared. At this point it became clear that as soon as the operators saw Joanna rolling in with the analyser, they upped their game and behaved themselves. And when she took the analyser away, they lapsed back into bad habits.

Joanna was able to do exactly what we had done with our Irish dairy clients. She would show the results from a week of monitoring. 'Your best day was here, your worst day was here. What's the difference? What happened? Is it a pump? Is it maintenance? Is it carelessness?'

We developed an app to enable dairy sales. Some of the information you needed to determine product losses could be pulled from the dairy's website. If you had the number of litres of milk they processed every year, and you knew how much BOD (biochemical oxygen demand) they produced, you could arrive at a figure very quickly.

And even if you allowed a huge margin of error, the potential savings as a result of installing BioTector were massive. With a big plant, it was always over a million euro, and with a smaller one, it was very rarely below €300,000. The ROI was literally a couple of months. Our highly expensive product was now as cheap as chips.

Between them, Andrew and Joanna amassed so much experience that we were able to show these plants exactly where their biggest vulnerabilities were, and how to go about reducing losses. We showed them how to track the numbers and use this to introduce process improvements. We could adjust the software to display BOD or TOC or litres of milk lost – whichever made the most sense for them to track. Tagging these weak spots, where milk might be lost, became part of BioTector training.

Some competitors did try to come in on our coat tails and made sales in this area, but they met all kinds of trouble and only ended up damaging their own reputations and enhancing ours. First of all, they had serious problems with false positives. An alarm would go off, everyone would come running but it would turn out that there was no leak, no spillage, no wasted product. That doesn't have to happen too often to turn people against an analyser. And of course these technologies couldn't deal with a sudden spike in raw product. If that happened, the analyser would have to go offline so that it could be cleaned out.

Sometimes we'd get pushed back on price. The customer would point out that Shimadzu and LAR analysers were about 10k cheaper. We'd say that in the context of the savings that were being made, this was an argument about pennies. "We're saving you €700,000 and you're talking about a €10,000 saving on the price of the analyser?"

The process manager had to have absolute confidence that the analyser was working, and he got that with BioTector. In fact, some of them asked Andrew to come in and calibrate the analyser every month, even though it only needed calibration twice a year. They wanted certification, something to prove that their safety net was fully functional.

We found then that we had a really high attachment rate. A customer who bought an analyser for product loss reduction reasons typically came back and bought five more. Here was proof of the value of these process applications over wastewater applications. You would only ever sell a single analyser for end of pipe reasons. Product loss reduction was essentially five times bigger than wastewater.

Moreover there were still industries – brewing and beverages – that we had yet to tap. This was ground breaking stuff and we had the market to ourselves.

Terry

We presented all of this to Terry, hoping that the numbers would bowl him over, hoping that he'd run off and set up a task force and blitz the dairy market. He didn't. He simply said that this would not be a runner in the US and that it didn't fit with the market as they saw it. Any time I was out for a drink with Terry, there was always a needle in the conversation. He might talk about what a great company LAR was, about how it was a great acquisition prospect.

I remember one time, we met him in Dublin and Mel was there to present all of the figures and the great marketing story we had built around the analyser, and about how well we were doing with System C. We were always super polite with Terry, always at great pains to acknowledge the wonderful job that Hach was doing and how delighted we were to have them on our side. Anyway, at this particular meeting Dad probably pushed a little too hard and Terry jumped up and slammed his fist down on the table. "I'm the head of a $20 million department and you're trying to tell me what to do?"

Our view was that he was blocking new products and new markets simply to exercise control, even though Hach could have been doing phenomenal business from dairy, from System C and so on.

Things got worse after that meeting.

Citing the fact that we were a competitor company, he began blocking all US sales information. So if Hach made a sale in the States, we were prevented from knowing who the customer was. Up to this point, if a Hach sales person needed help with a sale, he or she would simply get in touch with us directly and we'd fly over. Terry mightn't even know about the trip. Now, all travel to the US had to be sanctioned by him.

Now too, when an order came in from the US, we were instructed to send it to a centralised warehouse from where it would be rerouted to the customer site. This added a whole new layer of delay and complexity to logistics, and it appeared that the sole aim was to keep us out of the loop. Being blocked from all customer contact first in the US, then in Europe, was ridiculous and intolerable.

Ok, between myself, Dad and Jayne, we had great contacts within Hach who we could text and ask, "Where's that one gone?" – and they'd tell us, but really, this was no way to do business.

It became very clear that what we needed here was a Plan B. We were still building up our cash reserves, so that if sales fell off a cliff for any reason, we could continue to trade. Now too, we also started talking to integrators.

The Integrator

A little explanation is necessary here. In the normal course of events, the customer has a factory, he or she chooses the analyser needed and you go install it. With huge projects like Sadara, the process is different. They hire an integrator to purchase and integrate all of the required technology into prefabricated analyser houses. These are then shipped to the factory site, installed, tested and commissioned by the integrator. Integrators play a central role in huge global projects like Sadara. When BioTector was chosen, we suddenly appeared on the radar of a couple of these integrators, specifically ABB and Yokogawa. There was quite a bit of astonishment that a little-known Irish company of our size had been exclusively specified for such a big project.

The thing is, an integrator can also operate like a super-distributor. They tend to concentrate on new projects, and only ones of a certain size. So here's another route to the market. You could OEM (Original Equipment

Manufacturer) your technology, like Intel with Microsoft. You do a deal whereby every TOC analyser specified in a Yokogawa integration would be BioTector. So it's all Yokogawa's branding, but there would be a badge saying something like 'Includes BioTector'.

Because of our arrangement with Hach, we had decided not to go this route. Now that that relationship was getting increasingly complicated, we refocused our attention on integrators in general and Yokogawa in particular. The aim here was not to OEM our technology, but rather to explore a distributor arrangement in the Middle East.

We talked earlier about Ohmart VEGA being experts in industry but not in water, and Hach being experts in water but not so much in industry. Yokogawa ticked all the boxes – experts in both industry and in water. They were one of the main integrators on the Sadara project, so we began to have more and more dealings with them as the Sadara orders started to come in early in 2013.

Our Sadara analysers were sent to Yokogawa's US HQ in Texas, where they were installed in an analyser house before being shipped out to Saudi Arabia. The US president of Yokogawa happened to be based in the same building, so when I was out there inspecting the installation, I asked for a meeting with him.

To make the episode even more unusual, this trip was also one of the very few that Terry had sanctioned, so I spent most of it with Phil Landon, the sales guy for this area, and Jason Padilla, Hach's BioTector product manager, who had come down to meet me from Colorado. I had worked closely with these guys getting Hach up and running in the US, and by then we had developed a great relationship and were good friends. The morning of the Yokogawa meeting, I spent driving around to Hach customer sites with them, which is why I asked them to drop me to the meeting...and to wait in the car 'til I got back.

"It's all about Sadara," I explained, "it's confidential and outside your contract."

They were bemused, but they agreed to wait.

The president's office was the fanciest I had ever been in. Floor to ceiling oak panelling and a huge mahogany desk. I had wrangled a twenty minute slot and was told that this guy was exceptionally busy. So I went in, told him who I was and gave him the short version of how great BioTector was. I explained how our analysers had been specified across the whole Sadara project and suggested that Yokogawa become the BioTector distributor in the Middle East. Wouldn't it be handy, I said, if Yokogawa in the US shipped to Yokogawa in Saudi? BioTector could do all the training in both the States and the Middle East. It would be seamless.

He went for the idea straight away. Their plan had been to send trainers to Saudi with the shipment, guys who would then spend three months there getting everyone up to speed. With BioTector involved, that resource commitment would disappear. I asked for an introduction to the senior person in Yokogawa in the Middle East so that we could try to work something out. The US president agreed and a week later I was in a meeting with Pierre De Vust in Bahrain. He wasn't quite as enthused by the prospect of a deal with BioTector as was his colleague in the US, but as part of a distributor arrangement, we were offering the maintenance contract for the 100 Sadara analysers. This revenue stream was enough to convince him, so he agreed in principle to become the BioTector distributor for the Middle East.

Now, it was decision time.

Yokogawa was one of Hach's biggest competitors at the time. We knew that if we signed with them, we would be inviting direct conflict with the company that had enabled so much of our success. We knew that Hach's actions up to this point had been designed to scare us straight. They reasoned that if we knew we were jeopardising such a lucrative contract, we would immediately jump back into line. If we signed with Yokogawa, we would be saying that we were not afraid, that we were ready to face the consequences, and if those consequences included the loss of the contract, well, so be it. We were ready.

Dad and I were giddy talking about it. Are we really going to do it? Are we? Are we crazy? Terry is going to go ballistic. So we brought in the management team and laid it all out in front of them.

"Here's the story. You've seen what's going on. We're going to be negotiating a new contract with Hach in a years' time and we need to sort something out to give us back control. We want to be in charge of our own destiny." We pointed out that we had cash reserves and that if it all went pear-shaped and Hach dumped us, we could keep going, just as we had done when Ohmart VEGA pulled out. "If we lose Hach, we can come back stronger. We still have this great story to tell, we're still the best company in the world at doing this. Are we going to back ourselves?"

The management team said, "Yeah, let's do it!"

Before we took the plunge, I decided to conduct one more little test, basically to prove to myself that drastic action was necessary. As I've said, all of our distributors knew that the Sadara project was BioTector's exclusively, and that was fine. A situation cropped up in Belgium where a Hach Lange sales person, unaware of the Sadara clause, put in a good bit of time selling Bio-Tector to a Sadara integrator. There were three analysers involved. I got an email from Hach Lang as soon as somebody spotted what was going on. They referred the sale to us, but asked if there could be some sort of financial recognition for the work that they had done. Terry was copied in the email.

I was about to mail back saying that that was fine, we understood the mistake was made in good faith and that we recognised their great work and so on, but then I stopped. I had a brief chat with Dad about it, then I mailed back telling them that they needed to respect the contract, that Sadara sales were exclusively ours and that we'd take it from here. There would be no compensation for the work they had done.

That evening I got a phone call from Terry. "Who the hell do you think you are? I'm sick and tired of dealing with you. We've got a contract renegotiation coming up, and frankly I don't know if we will be renewing it."

I backed down immediately and said that of course

we would recognise the efforts of Hach Lange in facilitating the sale, but that phone call left me in no doubt about the difficulties we would have in the upcoming negotiation. Terry's tantrum had revealed exactly what he thought and how he would act when the contract renegotiation rolled around.

There's this phrase that Terry always used. "What game are we playing and how do we win?" What was clear now was that the game was contract renegotiation, and that the only way we could win was to have a plan B.

So we signed with Yokogawa, and I wrote the email.

Dear Terry
We wish to inform you that we have concluded an agreement with Yokogawa in the Middle East...

Chapter 9 - Stress

I got a text from Jason, my sales buddy in Hach. 'Have you guys done something? All the top brass are in a meeting in the boardroom. Everybody's very unhappy.'

I replied with, 'Just let me know when you hear.'

A couple of hours later, I got, 'YOU DID WHAT?'

Next thing myself and Dad were summoned to Hach HQ in Loveland, Colorado.

Crunch Meeting

Yokogawa was done. There was a contract in place and there was no going back on it. And I should say that contractually, we were entirely within our rights. There was nothing to stop us signing another distributor for an area not covered under the Hach contract.

And either of us – Hach or BioTector – could cancel at any moment. There was a process in place which allowed for the conclusion of sales and all that. Not that we wanted to cancel. And we hoped that they wouldn't cancel either. The Yokogawa contract was simply a way of strengthening our bargaining position ahead of the renegotiation, and of helping to realise our ambition to rebalance our sales away from Hach.

Myself and Dad got on a plane without any idea of what we'd meet on the other side. On the way, we discussed all kinds of scenarios and made all sorts of predictions about what Hach might say and so on. In all of this however we never anticipated what actually happened.

We were ushered into a meeting with the president and the vice-president. There was no sign of Terry anywhere. Nobody demanded to know what the hell we were playing at. "We see you've signed up with Yokogawa in the Middle East. We understand that that is not our territory and you're perfectly entitled to do that. We're just wondering what led you to this course of action."

Our story, which we stuck to, was simply that Yokogawa was the perfect Middle Eastern partner for us. We had worked closely with them on the Sadara project, so it was natural that we would formalise that contact with a distribution arrangement in Saudi Arabia and the Middle East. We also talked about some of the issues we had been having with Terry.

"We weren't aware of how bad things had gotten", they said, "but we understand we've been preventing you from contacting clients and stopping you from seeing where orders end up. We value our relationship with you. Frankly, we would have hoped that you would have reached out to us earlier if there were problems."

"This is your company," said Dad, "these are your employees. It's not up to us to explain to you what's happening. We assumed that what was going on was sanctioned by the company."

Straightaway we could see that we were dealing with an entirely different mindset. It was as if these guys had no idea what had been going on. They wanted to know what they needed to do to fix the situation, and immediately agreed to lifting the block on contact with customers. We were welcome once again to deal with Hach salespeople, while Robert Stevens would be free to visit with Hach Lange in Europe. Critically, they also agreed to look at launching System C.

The last thing we expected was that all of our problems would be sorted out in one fell swoop, but that's exactly what happened. Kevin Klau was the vice president who had led that meeting. He would, in time become the president of the company.

He said, "You have a direct line to me now. Any issues, you come straight to me and we'll resolve them. We value the relationship; we want to work towards the new contract." He told us that while they would have liked the

Middle East, Yokogawa were a great match for us. "Let's hold on to what we've got and build on that relationship."

We breathed a sigh of relief and flew home happy. The gamble had paid off.

Stress

As I said at the beginning, there's a risk in writing a story like ours that you give the impression that success was inevitable. It wasn't. Nor do I want to give the impression that the whole thing was easy or fun. There were moments of excitement and enjoyment certainly, but there were also periods of high stress, particularly during those months of conflict with Hach. I wouldn't be telling the full story if I didn't talk about these.

Sue was pregnant with our first child, Sarah, in the six months during which the relationship with Hach was at its most challenging. The prospect of becoming a father changes your perspective on things, and it also brings your choices into sharper relief.

I was still travelling all over the world and while this was exciting for me – two weeks in China just flew by – it was tough on Sue. She hated being in the house on her own. I'd always said, "Give me five years to get this sorted out." I figured that by then, we'd either have been acquired at a good price or earnings would be sufficient to hire more people to help out with the travel and/or the operational stuff. But after a while, the five year thing became meaningless. When exactly did it begin? And when would it end? Through all of this I was always conscious that I had made a commitment. Sarah was on the way. We would be a family and this way of life couldn't continue.

Anger

I felt huge anger towards Terry. As time went on, this anger took on a slightly obsessive tone. The thing is, I don't do heated exchanges well. I can't have shouting matches with people, I'm just no good at it. When these situations arise, I can't allow myself to lose my head, because I just don't perform well. My strategy, if you can call it that, is to just get through the situation as quickly as possible, then figure out the best thing to do after the dust has settled.

This sounds sensible but there are consequences. The first is that sometimes, people tend to underestimate me. The second, which is related to the first, is that I tend to self-recriminate. I get annoyed with myself for failing to engage. I do all that *when he said that, I should have said that* type of thing. I'm a plotter – I listen, I nod, I take it all in and I figure out how to act. This is playing to my strengths I suppose, but at the same time, I would have preferred to have been better at giving as good as I got.

Terry was exactly the type of person that I don't like dealing with because he's very confrontational. He's physically imposing and not shy about making his point. There were several incidents where he would rant and I'd sit there quietly and take it. Afterwards, it was very difficult not to endlessly replay the exchange in my head, coming up with better ripostes than I could think of at the time. And I just couldn't leave this stress in the office. I'd wake up in the morning with Terry on my mind, I'd go to sleep at night with Terry on my mind. My anger towards him became all-consuming. And it wasn't all an ego thing. I felt he was disrespecting Dad and everyone in our company.

There's another curious element to this. I did a training course a few years later and this question came up: "When did you perform at your peak, and what were the things that lead you to that?"

Whether it's a good or a bad thing, I realised that if I feel someone is underestimating me, that can act as a very powerful spur to my performance. When I look back over my life, I see that I excel when I'm up against someone. I might not be a skilled debater, but I am hugely competitive, and that streak provides a great deal of my motivation. The stress levels might have been high, but I knew I was performing really well.

The reality of course is that all of this obsessing was not a good thing. I was difficult to live with, I was causing myself a lot of grief and I worried too that the anger was distorting my decision making. Was I doing everything for the right reasons?

Presentations

The other problem was presentations. Because everything was coming together so well, I was making far fewer technical presentations, and far more sales presentations. The downside is that the technical presentations were easy. I was far more comfortable talking about the analyser to plant managers than I was talking about return on investment to those in more senior positions. Technical presentations are black and white. This is how it works, this is how it solves your problem. Value presentations focus on return on investment, are far more nuanced, require much greater persuasive skills and a different knowledge bank. I had no problem answering a technical question from a technical person, but the push back from more senior executives put me well outside my comfort zone.

Hach would set up webinars where there might be 300 people tuning in from all over the world and I would be there with my microphone and my slide deck trying to hold everyone's attention. For an introvert, for someone who doesn't have great natural ability in these situations, it was a very significant challenge.

The solution? Prepare, prepare, prepare.

And it worked. For that first big presentation, I put in huge amounts of time preparing and rehearsing, and in consequence, it went really well. So I did the same for the next presentation, and the next, and the next. Not just for presentations, but for meetings too. But the amount of time I was putting in was so great that it started to become a problem. It was unnecessary, it was over the top, it was a vicious cycle of over-prepare, do well, so over prepare again. Like my problems with Terry, it had an obsessive overtone. I couldn't simply let the meeting flow and trust myself to figure out how to act in the moment.

Things came to a head when we won the Frost & Sullivan Product Leadership award. Sue and I went to Knightsbridge in London for the presentation. Sue said, 'Just go up there and say thanks' but there were a lot of very senior people in the industry at the event, so I felt that this was another opportunity to sell our company. We had a captive audience, we were centre stage, we were being lauded for our product leadership. I felt I had to make the most of it. This meant however that I couldn't enjoy the trip. I spent all day preparing and was so nervous on the night that I couldn't eat the dinner. It was just a ten minute speech, but so much was sacrificed to make it as good as it could be. And it went really well, I got a great reception.

While Sue understood my motivation, the simple truth was that for the previous twenty-four hours, I was not an easy person to be around. Her point was simple. "You just can't put yourself through this all the time." And the result, good as it was, did not justify the amount of time I was putting in. All of the extra time wasn't actually *improving* the presentation, it was only an attempt to make myself feel better about it. On top of that, I was constantly doubting myself. I was meeting more and more senior people, and constantly thinking, 'Am I really good enough for this role?'

This was exacerbated by my tendency to never say 'no' to anything. If I felt it was good for the company, I'd sign up, then, when the day of the speech or the presentation or whatever it was finally arrived, I would think, *Oh God, Why did I commit to this?* I was making presentations to Enterprise Ireland, to other companies, to government ministers. Bricking myself before it, elated afterwards, and in that glow, signing up for the next thing, then bricking it again...It was an endless cycle.

I also had an unexpected reaction to adopting the CEO title. I always expected to take over from Dad – that had been the plan from the beginning – but I'd imagined that it would be as managing director. When it came to it, we chose CEO because we were a global company, and CEO was more universally recognised, but from the moment it went on my card, I hated it. I just didn't see myself as CEO material. You see them being interviewed on CNN. Six foot two, suave, well spoken, immaculately tailored suit and so on. That wasn't me.

Mervyn

Not only were we expecting our first child, there was also a bit of a baby boom going on in BioTector at the time. That too fed into my changing perceptions. I remember pulling into the car park in BioTector in the morning, and looking at everyone else going into work. I'd zero in on someone who'd just had a baby and think that I couldn't let him down. I had to make sure that the company would continue to thrive to keep him at work.

It was Sue who prompted me to go do something about it, to go and talk to somebody. She pointed out that I'd done courses on management and giving presentations and selling. Going to see a counsellor was the same. I needed a new set of skills. She made it seem like it was no big deal. "You're doing all these things to help your company, why not just do this as well? If it's rubbish you don't have to go anymore."

So I found this guy, Mervyn, and he was just great. He clarified that I wasn't responsible for everything. Sitting in the car and watching people going into work and feeling responsible for them, that wasn't my role. They had chosen to work in BioTector, and they could choose not to anytime they wanted. We treated them well, we paid them well, we gave them as much job security as we could but being there was their choice, not mine. My job is to make decisions. I do that to the best of my ability. I'll get things right and I'll get things wrong but allowing myself to be consumed by worry wouldn't help anyone.

I'd say something to Mervyn, and he would say, "I'm just going to repeat back to you and tell me how you think that sounds." And I'd hear the words I'd just used and be shocked by how, well, silly I sounded, how hard I was being on myself. Those conversations with Mervyn gave me back my perspective, so that when I did sign the Yokogawa contract, I was confident that I wasn't doing it just to piss Terry off. I was doing it for the good of the company.

Talking to somebody who's not going to judge you, who's not involved and who has a way of explaining things that, in the moment, you just weren't seeing clearly yourself, that was a liberating experience.

We agreed rules on presentations. For important meetings and presentations, ten hours prep for every hour on my feet. I do ten hours and say, right, I'm prepared. Anything beyond that, I'm not making it any better, all I'm doing is making my life miserable. And once I decided that I was prepared, there would be no need to think about it endlessly.

It worked. Not always, but usually.

Stress. Everyone has to deal with it, and some people just get on with it. I could have done that. I could have driven on and it probably would have worked out the same way but I made it a lot easier on myself by taking action and going to talk to someone. And if I was ever having an issue in the future, I'd have no problem going off and getting a bit of perspective on it.

There was one other thing I want to mention. I was

getting these episodes which I assumed were panic attacks. They would usually begin with a really strong sense of Déjà Vu and an uncertain dreamy sensation. This would last for about a minute then go, then come back, then go again. Often, there would be three 'waves' in succession, usually accompanied by nausea and a very strong taste in my mouth, as if I was about to vomit. These episodes, these sets of waves could last up to half an hour. If I could, I'd go somewhere and sit it out, but sometimes they would come on in a meeting. I'd just have to tell myself that I'd be alright, that it would stop.

I should have gone to the doctor straight away but I didn't. I decided – *panic attack, no time for that, get on with it, it'll be grand.* And I figured that these episodes would end when the situation with Hach got sorted out, but they didn't. So I went to the doctor.

It turned out to be a mild form of epilepsy called focal seizures, which can be brought on by stress and lack of sleep. Untreated, they can evolve into full epilepsy, but medication dealt with the symptoms very quickly and the problem disappeared.

The Approach
Anyway, the resolution of the Hach conflict had some

interesting consequences. Within Hach, there was a lot of surprise that we were able to do what we did. When I went on sales visits to Europe, they'd ask, "How did you get away with signing with Yokogawa? How did we let you do that?" The overwhelming reaction was unquestionably admiration. "Fair play," we were told, "that was the right move."

Outside of Hach, among our competitors, customers and other distributors, there was a lot of surprise. Everyone had been operating under the assumption that we had already been acquired by Hach, or that we were intertwined with them in some other fundamental way. Ours may be a global market, but it's still relatively small, and the deal we made with Yokogawa was big news. People said "You're not Hach? We thought you were Hach."

We were surprised at everyone's surprise, so we immediately amended all of our brochures, our marketing materials and our email footers, saying that we were an independently owned family company which made great analysers. So the conflict with Hach ended up having a significant positive impact on how we were perceived in the market.

When things happen in sequence, you always tend to link them, whether they're linked or not. In any case, a few months after all of this, Ali was at an industry event in the US. He was working with an expert group to help steer regulation and environmental standards. Ali, who holds a doctorate in chemistry, was perfect for this role. He travelled regularly to meetings, which, naturally enough, included a range of our competitors, including General Electric. Chatting with Ali, one of the GE guys asked him about the Yokogawa deal and our relationship with Hach. Ali explained that we were fully independent and that our agreements with Yokogawa and Hach were just standard distribution contracts. A week later, the GE guy got in touch with Ali and asked if he could set up a call between his boss and myself and Dad.

We didn't know what it was about of course, but we could guess. Either they wanted a distribution arrangement, or well, they were going to make an offer.

GE was a massive player in the industry. They had just brought out a rival product called InnovOx. It was based on a new technology, designed to make the analyser more robust. We had thoroughly researched it and had concluded that the product itself was nowhere near as good as BioTector. GE had such sales and marketing muscle of course that even if the product itself wasn't up to our standards, they could still make inroads into the market.

Anyway, this call coincided with the birth of our daughter, Sarah. Not only that but the day she was born, we heard our offer for the site on which we would build our house had been accepted. The following day, I remember leaving Sue in the hospital to come back to the office to take the call from GE, which was on Skype – the first time we'd ever used it. So there was all the usual stuff when you use one of these technologies for the first time. *Is the camera on or off? Sorry, we can't hear you*! And all that.

Once everything was settled, Dave Jellison, the head of GE's water analysis division introduced himself. He asked if myself and Dad were the only ones in the room.

"Yes, it's just us."

"I'm going to get straight to the point. We want to buy your company."

Dad said exactly what he said back when Hach first made their approach. We're flattered, but we were not for sale. Dave said that he understood that but asked if he and a couple of his colleagues could fly over to discuss the possibility.

"I have to ask," he said, "are you tied in with Hach in any way? Are you free to deal?" We told him the truth, which was that there was a right of first refusal clause in our agreement with Hach. If anyone made an acceptable acquisition offer, Hach had the right to buy at that price. "Ok," said Dave, "that would be typical of a distribution contract of that size, it isn't a barrier. So will you meet us?"

We said that we would.

This was June of 2013, three months after we had signed Yokogawa. Were the two events connected? I'm inclined to believe that they were. There was so much talk about us at that time; the clarification that we were independent probably set people thinking.

The Team

Sometimes, one of our employees would ask directly if we were going to be acquired. We were doing great, we were winning awards, we were the type of company that tended to be acquired. I always answered in the same way. I said that we were the best in the world at what we did and that any company would be lucky to get us. So do I expect approaches in the future? Yes, I do. Do I think anyone is going to value the company the way we do? No, I don't. And that was honest. Our experience with the original Hach offer had led myself and Dad to the conclusion that no one really got how good we were. So while it was nice to be entertaining a giant like GE, we were fairly confident that they'd never come up with a price that we would be able to accept.

I was 34 or 35 at the time. I figured that we could continue on this wonderful trajectory that we were on well into the future, that we were only getting better at what we did. There was no reason to sell. Having said all that, we were now a very different proposition compared to what we had been when Hach first approached us four years earlier. We were poised to realise the fantastic potential we knew we had.

Ahead of the visit, myself and Dad agreed that while he would be there for all of the meetings, it would make more sense for me to do most of the presenting. Why? Because part of the value of the company lay in the fact that I could remain in place to keep running it. An acquiring company could replace me obviously, but if that wasn't an option, they would need someone that would be willing to stay the course, and Dad was on the point of retiring.

Those two days with GE were almost perfect. From the moment we picked them up at the airport until we dropped them back, everything just worked. As we went through the presentations and showed them everything we had done, all of the work around dairy, and how it applied to a list of other industries, they actually appeared shocked. They told us that they knew we had a great product, but they had no idea about the strategy. We were able to demonstrate, in clear, compelling terms, how the market we were operating in was between five and six times bigger than the market they were operating in. We explained how our analyser was uniquely suited to corner this market and that no other analyser – including InnovOx – could compete. We had the story. We had the strategy. The huge growth we'd clocked up in the previous four years was only the beginning. We were alone in a market that was so big that there was no reason why the growth trajectory could not continue for years to come. Ok, we had only proven the dairy argument, but GE, a \$100bn company with a presence in so many sectors, could readily source figures from all those other industries. Moreover, they could accelerate our growth plan at a far greater rate than we ever could, even with Hach on our side.

It was clear from very early on that they bought it. They saw, as clearly as we did, what could be done with BioTector. We spent most of our time over those two days talking about potential and market size and what sales might look like in five years' time. It was perfect.

A few days later, the GE people rang up to say that they had been hugely impressed by their visit and that they wanted to make a formal bid for BioTector.

Chapter 10 – Acquisition

Acquisition, the possibility of acquisition is a very sensitive subject. We didn't have the freedom to talk openly about GE's offer in the office, so here again was another job that Dad could slot into. By now, he had moved into an office upstairs, away from everyone else, and could talk freely on the phone without the fear of being overheard and starting rumours. The door of my office was always open. If I started closing it, it would seem odd. It would give rise to the kind of speculation that we wanted to avoid. So this whole period was tricky and needed a lot of management.

It was up to GE to come up with a number, but we felt that we couldn't just leave it at that. We wanted to make sure whatever they came up with was based on real data. We needed a document – a prospectus really – something that detailed what we were all about; our story, our culture, our product leadership position; everything. And, on the last page, there would be a number which we felt represented the true value of the company.

Myself and Dad couldn't do this on our own. We needed help from our marketing expert, Mel and financial controller Margaret. By this time, we had identified

Margaret as a person who could take on a kind of COO role if and when I opted to reduce my time in the office. She was very smart, very hungry to learn. She understood how the company worked and knew the figures inside out. So Margaret, Mel and Dad were the acquisition taskforce. They invited O'Kelly Sutton to come in and create the document we needed. The taskforce provided the story and Pat Sutton – Paul O'Kelly's partner in the business – and his team worked up the figures and framed the prospectus in the appropriate way.

The Price

If we found GE's offer acceptable, we were obligated to take it straight to Hach, who would have eight weeks to either match it or let us go. This dynamic had an unexpected and very positive benefit for us. Because GE was so keen to buy, it was in their interest to make whatever offer they made unattractive to Hach. For this reason, they explored all of the ways they could optimize the value of the company, without, of course, making us appear overvalued to their own management, who would have to sign off on the deal.

The timing of GE's approach could hardly have been better. The final price would be based around our

EBITA (earnings before interest, tax, depreciation and amortisation) for 2013. We'd grown our sales fivefold since 2010, and on top of that, Sadara related sales came flooding in 2013. A multiplier would then be applied to this figure; the size of that would be dependent on a range of variables, including the strength of our projections.

If all you had was a great product, that's all you could talk about, but what became clear during this phase was that companies like GE and Hach don't buy great products, they buy great companies. They want great management teams, great people, great vision and strategy, great processes, procedures and compliance. Gaining access to a good technology is one thing, but the reality is that they will pay more for a company that's gone through the hard graft of making itself great. And all of that work added significantly to the multiplier and therefore the value of the company. Without these things, it would have been much more difficult for the GE acquisitions team to go back and credibly argue that we were worth what we were asking.

Moreover, because GE was so keen to buy us, we were spared a lot of the hassles small companies usually have to deal with when they're being acquired. Usually, when a big company comes in and tries to acquire you, you agree a price, then, after the fact, they starting introducing all kinds of provisos designed to protect themselves and ultimately drive the price lower. An earn-out is a good example. The buyer might agree to pay 50% of the agreed price upfront, and the other 50% in, say, five years, if pre-agreed earnings targets are reached. The earn-out is like an insurance policy, and it would have been a standard feature of many acquisition agreements. GE made sure that their offer included a 100% upfront payment, with no earn-out, no dependent targets, thereby making the deal that bit less attractive to Hach.

Despite Dad's previous experience selling Irish Superior, there was a lot we didn't know, a lot that GE explained to us. They kept coming up with concessions that they knew Hach would hate, all the time trying to make the offer so favourable towards us that it would never be accepted by their opposite numbers in Hach. Someone would say, 'Let's put that in. We'd hate that!' It was bizarre really, and a fascinating insight into how big companies structure deals like these.

In addition to O'Kelly Sutton's help with the prospectus, we also took valuable advice from Ernst and Young and from our own external accountant, Adrian Galvin. But, as I say, there was no real negotiation at this point. They had our document, they knew what we were looking for, and they had their own acquisition process. The acquisition team had to ensure a return on investment within a set period in order to get sign off. Most of the negotiation, if you can call it that, was GE asking for more time so that they could secure a higher number and make it less likely that Hach would go for it. And in the end, the number they came up with was actually very close to the one we had specified in our prospectus.

Other bidders?

We also explored the idea of getting Bank of Ireland involved. They had a specialist acquisitions advisory unit who came in and presented to us. They pointed out that we were a small company, that acquisitions were very complicated, that we didn't understand them and that companies like Hach and GE did acquisitions for breakfast. When it came to a negotiation, they would chew us up. Bank of Ireland offered to broaden the market, to bring in five or six additional bidders. We thought about it but in the end, we decided against that approach.

We felt that we knew our company and our technology inside out. We believed that we could handle it. I would have to say too that we felt a certain loyalty to

GE. That might sound crazy but they had treated us very fairly, we were happy with how the process was evolving and we felt that suddenly bringing in three more bidders just wouldn't be right. And if we went more aggressively into the market place, we would have transformed from a company being pursued by a buyer to one pursuing a buyer, and we didn't want that. If it fell through at that point, everyone would know that the company had been up for sale – your staff, your distributors, your suppliers. It could be damaging. As it stood, we were able to manage the process discreetly. If a deal failed to happen, it would not have been a tragedy. We were working away, doing great things on our own, and there was no reason to believe that that would change.

Before we accepted the GE offer, we got together as a family to chat about it, to make sure no one had any reservations. Dad made the point that we could continue to work on alone as before, that the company was very healthy and would be in a position to pay dividends to shareholders over the coming years. It was agreed however that the offer was simply too good to refuse. It would be very many years before we could ever recoup a figure like that.

The offer goes to Hach

So GE made their offer and we conditionally accepted it. Straightaway Dad picked up the phone and called Kevin Klau, the vice president of Hach. His reaction? He actually congratulated us. "Well done," he said, "you've achieved a great value for your company."

This shows just how much better the relationship had become in the months since our trip to Loveland. And of course companies like GE and Hach are well used to acquisitions. It's a far less personal business for them than it was for us. This was massive in our lives, but not in theirs, so it was good of him to acknowledge what we had achieved.

"We now have eight weeks to evaluate this," said Kevin. "We'll be flying over to talk to you. Can you make yourselves available?"

We said that of course we would. At this point, we believed that the price would simply be too high for them. And I have to say that we loved the fact that GE totally got what we were saying about the market and our position in it. We had more or less convinced ourselves that Hach would pass and GE would buy. I was having a cup of coffee one day, thinking all of this through and

I realised that actually, no. Hach would buy. They would have to. I remember going up to Dad and explaining my thinking. "If you play through the scenarios, there's just no way they're going to let a major competitor take away all the work they've done. They just won't do it. Hach are going to buy us."

Even if they didn't see the same value in us as GE did, they would ask themselves, well, why don't we see it? Up to this point, because we had convinced ourselves that Hach would reject the offer, we had not put as much effort into promoting the company as we had for GE. Now, we realised that this wasn't a good idea, so we kicked into gear and created a new draft of the O'Kelly Sutton prospectus. We had to change the emphasis, we had to acknowledge Hach's input and their existing knowledge of the company. Not a major rewrite, but enough so that we could be seen to be even-handed in our approach.

Shortly after Kevin's visit, Dad took a call from Lance Reisman, who was then the president of Hach. He talked about what a good fit Hach was for BioTector, and how, if we were acquired by Hach, it would be a much smoother transition for everybody. While he didn't come right out and say this, Dad's impression was that Hach would struggle to reach the price GE had set, and that

Lance was preparing the ground for a lower counter offer. Dad understood what he was saying, and it was true, it would be an easier transition if it was Hach rather than GE, but he still rang Kevin and let him know that we would not entertain a lower offer. Hach had to match it.

Hach's eight week window fell over Christmas of 2013. In the end, because of this, they actually got nine weeks – a fact that GE were more than a little annoyed about. GE had to pull out all of the stops to get authorisation for so high an offer, and they naturally felt that if Hach got sufficient time, they would have a better chance of getting the authorisation they would need. Whatever internal wrangling happened over Christmas, Kevin Klau flew back to see us in early January with an offer. They matched the price. Hach would buy us.

Timing

Dad rang GE to let them know. Were they disappointed? Dad's impression was that they were so big, and did so many of these acquisitions that really, it was no big deal. You win some, you lose some. They congratulated us and said that if anything went wrong at the due diligence stage, to get in touch and maybe we could discuss things further.

Here's another interesting point about the timing

of all of this. It was the head of GE's water division, Dave Jellison, who kicked off the acquisition. He was hugely enthusiastic about the possibility of acquiring BioTector. Once he got that process going, GE's acquisitions team took over, but without that key advocate within the company, we would never have achieved the price that we had. In fact, the whole thing might not have happened at all. Dave actually left the company not long after the acquisitions team had taken over. So if we had delayed, or gone looking for other bidders, there's every chance that GE would have withdrawn. The timing of the approach, and our rapid response to it turned out to be critical to its success.

There was good timing too in relation to our first patent. You get a patent for twenty years, and ours was due to run out in 2020. This was in 2014, so two thirds of that time had elapsed. While we were making up our own minds, we were always conscious of the fact that once our strongest patent ran out, there was a risk that one of our competitors might try to copy us. Even if they were successful, they still mightn't do a very good job – they certainly wouldn't understand the technology as well as we did. Moreover, we had also taken out a series of additional patents which were designed to make copying the technology more difficult when that first one ran out. However, if someone chose to copy our original design, there was a risk that they could advertise the fact that they had an analyser which used the market leading technology. The value of the strongest patent therefore declined the closer we came to that expiry date.

Due Diligence

Both offers, from GE and from Hach, were subject to due diligence. This is an involved, costly process, which is only undertaken by the successful bidder. It began in January 2014 and continued for three months.

Mom and Dad, as I say, had gone through a process like this before, when Irish Superior was acquired by Chubb. Their experience here made a big difference. They had set the company up in the first place with one eye on the possibility of acquisition down the road, so everything was recorded, everything was tracked, everything was on file.

Acquiring companies arrive into small companies and expect to see gaps and omissions. They see that they will have to implement procedures, and at a certain cost, and that undermines the value. If the list of these gaps and omissions is too long, the value will be eroded, sometimes to the point where it no longer makes sense to buy. By contrast, thanks to the efforts of Mom, Mel and Margaret, we were able to hand over a varied selection of packs – on standard operating procedures, marketing, financials, health and safety, regulation compliance, sales forecasts, market positioning and so on. Vincent also played a significant role in this.

Vincent

Back in 2011, the government brought in a programme called JobBridge. Companies could employ someone on social welfare for nine months. They retained their benefits and got an additional allowance, and if everything worked out, they would go on the payroll. The scheme got a lot of negative publicity but it worked out brilliantly for us. As I've said before, my view is that the interview is a flawed means of working out someone's suitability for a job, but if you work alongside a candidate, you find out quite quickly whether or not they're going to fit in. In all, we availed of JobBridge six times, and ended up offering five people jobs as a result. One person chose not to take it up, but in any case, they had proved the need for someone in that role, so we went out and hired someone else.

One guy in particular worked out wonderfully. One

of Vincent's most recent jobs had been in the toll booth on the Fermoy by-pass. We were able to see from very early on that he was hugely capable. He had tremendous knowledge and understanding of processes and procedures. We actually ended up promoting him twice in a very short space of time, during which he slotted into a key oversight role straddling several different sections of the company.

His job was to oversee documentation relating to production; ensuring we had proper procedures in place, following 5S, complying with health and safety and all of that. He also worked with R&D to ensure existing products and those in development complied with RoHS (Restriction of Hazardous Substances) and REACH (Registration, Evaluation, Authorisation and Restriction of Chemicals). These are onerous compliance protocols which small companies typically find difficult to implement. Because Hach were and are extremely conscientious about this stuff, the fact that we had them in place was a significant mark in our favour.

Vincent's role, and the way in which he documented these procedures became very significant during the due diligence process because we were simply able to hand over his files to demonstrate how well we had complied.

Vincent had a little saying that I'd hear from

time to time. If rumours came up – as they did during this phase – he'd throw his hands in the air and say, "Let managers manage." And that tended to bring an end to the speculation.

Discretion

At this point, it was very hard to keep the due diligence from our colleagues. The acquisitions team went through everything with a fine tooth comb – accounts, certifications, production stuff, standard operating procedures, health and safety records...There was no section of the company that was not forensically analysed.

People became increasingly suspicious. When Mel or Margaret or Dad came in to my office to talk about something, we'd frequently close the door. You could get away with it by saying, 'Oh, it's HR stuff,' but that loses credibility after a while. We had meetings in the International Hotel near the airport, but again, I'd have to justify why I was out of the office for three hours. My brain was fried, trying to manage things and keep it quiet. If it wasn't for Dad working away in his corner office at the top of the building, it would have been impossible.

So the due diligence process was a pain but we were well prepared for it. And an acquisition team is like any other group of human beings. They come in to do a job and they hope that it's not going to be difficult or tedious. They hope they're not going to run into obstacles. The fact that we were able to deliver everything on their checklists quickly and without fuss made their lives so much easier. We were told that they hadn't met this level of organisation or preparedness in a company of our size before. It's no harm to have that kind of feedback filtering back up the line to the person who'll be writing the cheque. 'Yes, this company is great – you should definitely acquire them.' It was as if we had recruited them to advocate internally for us.

Over the course of these sessions, we would frequently be asked the same questions in a slightly different way, just to make sure – it seemed – that we were telling the truth. The acquisitions team had an accountancy mindset. They wanted straight, factual answers, without any embellishment. They loved Seamus for this reason. If they asked myself or Dad a technical question about the analyser, we would invariably go off into explanations about why this particular feature was so good. Seamus, by contrast, would answer simply and precisely without any hint of marketing.

Mel and Margaret and Mom also did an outstanding

job throughout this phase. They addressed the continuous stream of queries that flowed in, tracked all of the data and updated the schedules as necessary.

Grey areas

I was surprised at just how important our solicitor was in the deal. You always think that things are black and white, that there's a right way and a wrong way, but there's actually a lot of grey. In many of the contract negotiations, there would be three or four solicitors acting on behalf of Danaher on one side of the table, and all of them would have years of acquisitions experience. On the other side, there would be me, Dad and our solicitor, Ray. He was just great. He understood everything and pushed back whenever it was needed, while most of the time, myself and Dad just sat there watching.

Ray was particularly skilled at navigating those grey areas. There were all kinds of issues – around warranties, how we would handle cash in the company, how we would handle stock and analysers in production and so on. By progressing through each thing slowly and methodically, he was able to make such clear points that the guys on the other side of the table would look at each other and go, 'Ok, yeah, he's right'. They'd concede and move on to the next thing. He batted away so many complications with clear thinking and even clearer explanations. He made me realise what a terrible solicitor I'd make because I'd have to go away for a week to think about it, then go and write an email.

Vision

I mentioned before that having a vision, a mental picture of a goal fulfilled has always been really useful for me. During the acquisitions process, I developed my own vision of what success would look like. It helped to clarify where it was going, what we were trying to do. That image was simply myself and Susie sitting down with her parents and telling them that we had been acquired, that we'd done well and that the day wasn't far away when I wouldn't have to travel any more. That's the little video that would play over and over in my head, that's what resonated with me and helped to keep me focused on the work.

Why not my own family? My own parents and brothers? I suppose we all grew up with constant travelling, with the understanding that this was how you grew the family's wealth, this was how you grew a company. No explanation was necessary. But I always wondered how Sue's family felt about my frequent absences. They knew she hated being at home alone, and now of course Sarah had arrived. Throughout the first year of her life, I was up to my neck in the business and the acquisition, so my time at home was very limited. Sue's parents – Aggie and Kevin – were wonderful, they were a constant source of support and help for Sue. And because they were there so much at that time, they formed a great bond with Sarah. But it can't have been easy to see their daughter and granddaughter on their own for much of the time.

That simple image really helped to keep me motivated through the hectic comings and goings that characterised this phase. It's funny. This process of visualisation has always worked really well for me, so much so that I'm sometimes shocked by how these images I've created actually come to pass. One of the big things for me when I was a kid was Gaelic football. I always imagined myself running out on the pitch wearing a Cork jersey. I was small and light as a player, but I was handy enough. And it actually came to pass in 2002. I made the Cork championship panel. I think I was actually playing better football in 1997 and '98, and maybe I deserved it more then, but it didn't happen. It was only the Cork juniors, but it still happened, and it was weird when it did. This image I had in my head for so long actually happening in real life.

Announcement

The due diligence turned up no surprises and Hach made a formal offer, which of course we were obliged to accept.

The deal was done. BioTector had been sold.

The next step was to break the silence and tell everyone. Danaher was great at this stage. Because they do acquisitions all the time, they have a very well structured programme in place to facilitate the handover. They understand that events like these generate a lot of shock and anxiety, so the announcement, and the hundred-day plan that followed it, were designed to reassure everybody. To help mitigate the shock, the acquisitions team planned to introduce a range of perks, which included salary increases and a health insurance pack.

A huge level of work went into the day of the announcement itself. We had to sort out salaries, pensions, how the existing bonuses worked and so on. I had a presentation to give, and naturally enough I put a lot of time into making sure it was exactly right. The plan was that we would gather everyone together and explain what was about to happen. Hach would not be in the room. They would wait downstairs, and once I had done my piece, they would come in, take over and begin their own process of reassuring everyone, explaining the perks and detailing the plan.

So much effort went into that one day. Countless hours of preparation by dozens of people, all centred on easing the transition from us to them. And yet, somehow, nobody spotted that the day we had chosen for all of this was April 1st. April fool's day. We couldn't quite believe that we had allowed it happen, but by the time it was spotted, it was too late to pull out. When I stood up to make my presentation, the first thing I had to say was that this was real. It wasn't an elaborate prank.

The Reaction

I knew in advance that not everyone would welcome the news. There was one guy on the team who had worked for a company that Danaher had taken over. They had immediately shut the company down and moved it to the far side of the globe. For that reason, Rob had always been wary of Hach and its parent, and it was he, more than anyone else, who would ask if we were likely to be acquired. My answer, as I've said before, was that Hach, or any buyer, would be lucky to get us, but that it was unlikely they would see our value as we did. The minute

I delivered the news, Rob had his head in his hands. One of the students we had working in the R&D lab burst out crying. She had only been in the company a couple of weeks.

So it was very difficult, standing there, trying to keep the whole thing positive. I was glad to hand over to Kevin who had been waiting patiently downstairs for the call to come up and start talking. He was great, he did a brilliant job. His background is HR, and he's a gifted communicator. Very empathetic, great with people. He spoke about everyone's concerns, he detailed all of the good stuff that would happen and answered all of the questions with which he was bombarded.

Afterwards, we went downstairs for pizza and the questions and talking went on in a more informal way. But it was still very stressful. Despite all of the reassurances, people were understandably anxious. I had a queue of people into the office to quiz me up and down on what lay ahead. On that note, the preparation paid off really well. We had detailed a long list of likely questions and had made sure that all of the answers were as clear and as detailed as possible, so we weren't blindsided by anything.

Naturally enough, the big worry was that BioTector would move to China the following day. It took a lot of talk, a lot of explanation to convince people that that wasn't going to happen. And the truth was that regardless of what we said, this was always going to be an emotional, uncertain time. People were genuinely worried. I think on that first day, many of them weren't really listening to what was being said, they were just trying to digest the news. And there was no way to prove to them that all of their concerns were unfounded. You just had to listen and repeat what you knew, what you believed was likely to happen. It would take time for them to absorb the truth, which was that BioTector was going nowhere.

And it didn't go anywhere. The company continues to operate at full capacity in Cork, though further growth prompted a move to a bigger premises.

We had always known that whoever bought us – GE or Hach – it made zero sense to shut down any part of the factory. We were doing things to a very high standard on a very niche product, and it simply wouldn't be possible to achieve that standard anywhere else. Moreover, this was a high margin product. Moving to a low wage economy just to squeeze an extra few percent out of the margin simply wouldn't make sense. Hach's strategy, we could see, was just to sell more. Production would gear up like never before and they would drive sales even higher. And that's exactly what happened.

But of course you never know what will happen. Barely a year later, GE sold its entire water division to a company called SUEZ. So despite our ambivalence between GE and Hach, it would turn out that if Hach had been unable to match the GE price and we had sold to GE, it would have been a disaster. A lot of people couldn't understand why we sold at all. From their point of view, things were going great, and only getting better, so they couldn't see the rationale. Because we were restricted from talking about the price at the time, we couldn't bring that up. I just had to say that having evaluated everything, selling made sense for myself, Mom and Dad and our families. We had put so much in over the last twenty years and now seemed like the right time to move on.

The acquisition completed on March 28th 2014 with the announcement four days later on April 1st.

In four and a half years, the value of the company had gone from €2.65 million to almost €45 million. Four and a half years since Hach first put in their original offer, since our accountant told us that actually, €2.65 million was a fair price. That's an increase of nearly 1600%.

And the conversation with Sue's parents happened just as I had imagined. We had lunch together and told them that we had signed the documents, that BioTector was being sold. They were delighted for me, for us.

Chapter 11 - Aftermath

Hach spent three days launching their one hundred day plan in BioTector, then I left to begin a tour of customers and distributors to tell them about the new arrangement. This meant that in the phase immediately after the announcement, travelling for myself and Robert Stevens actually increased.

I was accompanied on the first of those visits by Kevin Klau and Hach president Lance Reisman. This was to Yokogawa. I had thought that their contract would be the first to be torn up when Hach took over, but no. They saw the value in the relationship. From there, I went on to visit some of the existing distributors that Hach had elected to hold onto, as well as unfamiliar Hach locations in Thailand and India.

And back in the office, the management team was busy keeping the hundred-day plan moving, keeping everything positive. In my absence, they had a critical role here. Hach had pointed out that they would be under close scrutiny in the weeks following acquisition, and that if the senior team appeared anxious or unsettled, that would send ripples of unease through the company.

Kaizen

One of the great things they did, almost immediately, was to stage a Kaizen event. These are short-duration improvement drives, which Hach used to demonstrate how good they were at processes and procedures, and how committed they were to keeping the company in Cork. They brought in experts from Germany who worked with our team to transform the warehouse. At the time our stores were packed and we were on the point of giving the go head for the construction of a mezzanine to create more space. Hach said, 'Hang on, let's take another look'. In the space of a week, these experts rearranged both our processes and our stores so ingeniously that there was no need for the building work.

It was one of these very quick, very visual wins that set everyone talking. 'How did they do that so fast? It's fantastic!' This helped a lot in winning hearts and minds and letting everyone know that these guys were capable, they knew what they were doing, and especially that they were there for the long-term. You're not going to invest resources and energy if your secret plan is to decamp to China in six months.

In advance of signing, we made a gentleman's

agreement that I would continue to work as MD for the company for the following two years. Dad stopped being an employee immediately but agreed to stay on as a consultant for a set number of days a month. Mom, meanwhile, took the opportunity to retire.

I absolutely loved that first year.

Why? I have to say that Kevin Klau had a big role to play. He went on, as I say, to be president of Hach, and since then he's become quite senior in the broader Danaher organisation. He was hugely impressive. He was great to work with and had a fantastic leadership style. I think I worked as hard during that first year as I did at any other time, and much of that was down to the fact that Kevin was such a great motivator.

He made sure that I was among a handful of people picked to go on an accelerated leadership programme within Danaher. That was an amazing experience. I also spent a lot of time on the phone with Kevin and the Hach leadership team, learning how corporations strategise and manage teams. He brought me into high level planning meetings as an observer, and again, these were a fantastic learning experience. Kevin was all about trust and guidance and putting people first. 'You sell the vision, then you trust people to deliver on it and support them along the way.'

It was actually quite embarrassing, because when our son was born, we called him after Sue's dad, Kevin. This became a big joke around the office. When Kevin Klau asked what we had called him, I had to quickly explain that he was named after his grandad.

I felt that one of my key roles throughout this period was to keep reinforcing the message: Hach was here to stay. I'd tell everyone about the great things they were doing in the US, the great things they were doing in Japan. I'd tell them the stories which proved that Hach wanted to grow our business and wanted to grow it in Cork. Frankly, I never questioned that. The acquisition process had proved to me that they walked the walk as well as talking the talk. They did what they said they would do.

Dad was amused by all this. "You've bought into this whole thing, you're singing off the same hymn sheet as them." And it was true, I was. Danaher Business Systems – which I had been suspicious of back when we first negotiated a distributor contract – now made sense to me. So I loved that first year, there was no sense of 'I can't wait to get out of here', none at all. Yes I was travelling a lot, and I knew that was a problem, but I was learning so much.

As that year came to an end, Kevin asked me if I'd

consider taking on a new role in Hach. TOC Business Unit Manager.

I ended up turning the job down, but I have to say I was thrilled to be asked. I would have been looking after BioTector and all of the other TOC analysers that Hach had on their books. And that included Astro. You'll remember one of our strategic goals in the 2010 strategy was to kill Astro. Well, it finally came to pass. In 2014, Hach announced that they were discontinuing the Astro, beginning in Europe and the US.

Operational Excellence

BioTector was a product leadership company. Hach is an operational excellence company. Great procedures, great ways of doing things. Through the transitional phase, BioTector slowly began to conform to the Hach way of doing things. Back when our focus was on product leadership and innovation, we were implicitly choosing to neglect other things, because you can't be good at everything. So despite all the improvements we had made, we weren't as good at procedures and processes as we could have been. It was a choice we had made. That was all changing. Excellent processes and procedures were imposed. And conversely, many of the things we used to do stopped. No more pet projects in R&D. No more doing whatever the customer wanted. From then on, tweaks and adaptations would only be implemented if they could demonstrate a clear ROI.

Those in the company who were operationally focused – people like Margaret, Ian and Vincent – blossomed in this environment. They loved all of the process innovations coming in from Germany and beyond.

Different parts of the company now took their lead from different parts of Hach. Production was being advised from Germany. Margaret too was getting direction on finance from Germany. Seamus was directed from a fantastic group based in the US. Everything was more controlled, more process-oriented, more methodical, and everyone with that kind of mindset loved it.

Inevitably of course there were those who didn't see things in quite the same light. The likes of Ali, who would always bend over backwards for the customer, he wasn't mad about it. Those who loved the pet projects and the figuring things out, they struggled. They felt they were being buried in paperwork.

Year Two

Over dinner and during coffee breaks on that accelerated leadership programme, we sometimes talked about home and family. One thing that all of these senior people bemoaned was the fact that they rarely saw their families. They were on their own the whole time. They were always travelling and they always tended to be under fierce pressure. And yet they loved their jobs and were hoping to get to more senior positions in the Danaher organisation.

So sending me on that programme kind of backfired on Kevin. It was brilliant, it was hugely motivational and in many ways I'd have loved to have continued, but I realised that the timing was wrong. I had to put my family first. So, after the end of that first year, I rang Kevin and told him that while I really enjoyed it, and was honoured to be asked to stay on, I would be leaving at the end of the second year. I explained my thinking and he got it.

"You could have said nothing and just taken the new position because it would have looked good on your CV, but knowing this early allows me to go find the right person...Those demons in your head, I hear them all the time too and someday I hope I listen to them."

Once I'd made the decision to pass on the new opportunity, it was like a switch had flipped. The second year was much more difficult. The transition had gone smoothly and I had no guiding vision anymore, no compelling reason to be there. I had given my word that I would stay on, but my heart was no longer in it. Kevin had asked me not to broadcast the fact that I would be leaving as planned, but people could probably see that I wasn't bringing the same level of enthusiasm to things.

Motivation

Hach were excellent motivators. They were very quick to retain and reward talent. So very soon after the acquisition, Margaret took over the financial controller role in a number of other Hach companies. Seamus was given a research role in collaboration with the Tyndall Institute in Cork, and he really enjoyed that.

Nobody left the company as a result of the acquisition. I think one person left within that two-year window, but for reasons unrelated to Hach's arrival. Myself and Dad were the first ones to actually resign.

How did that feel? Was I sad? Well, no, not at all. Driving out on that last day, I remember a feeling of contentment. BioTector didn't need me anymore. While I might have been useful, I was no longer necessary. My role had diminished and devolved to different parts of the Hach organisation in different parts of the world.

The management team was now good enough to grow the company and bring it to a higher place without us. Everyone was thriving, things were great. There was a real sense of completeness. The work here is done. I did the best I could for the ten years I was there, and Dad did amazing things over the twenty-two years he was there, and now both of us could walk away knowing we weren't leaving anyone in the lurch.

Realising a vision

Enterprise Ireland had an inward investment programme where, if there was a multinational you were particularly targeting, they would pay for them to visit your factory and your customers, on condition that they also visit a number of other Irish companies. It was a fantastic programme and we made use of it to bring Lactalis over. They are a big dairy company to whom we'd already sold a few analysers. That visit went really well, and culminated with me travelling to Paris and meeting up with a couple of Hach corporate people. From there, we took a train down to the little town where Lactalis was head quartered and met with their sustainability people.

Back during that first ever strategy session, the day I began working in BioTector, Paul O'Kelly had painted his vision of success. I would be wearing a suit and walking into corporate HQ to meet senior corporate people. I wouldn't be talking technology, I wouldn't be talking about valves and pumps. I would be making a compelling argument about return on investment, and at the end of that meeting, BioTector would be specified in 200 factories across the entire organisation. And on this, my very last BioTector trip, that is exactly what happened. I don't think I mentioned TOC once in the presentation. It was all about product loss prevention and return on investment. We signed a pricing agreement with Lactalis selecting BioTector as their analyser of choice across their 200 plus plants worldwide. The whole thing corresponded so closely to that vision I had retained throughout that time. It was uncanny.

Though we never trumpeted our environmental credentials, we had always been an environmentally aware company. That was reflected in our original name – Pollution Control Systems – and of course the fact that the analyser existed in the first place to prevent contaminants from escaping. Over time BioTector evolved from a means of preventing pollution to a management tool for loss prevention. In that transition however, it actually became a more powerful weapon against pollution. By preventing leaks and losses early in the production process, way less pollutants were getting to the end of the pipe. Less contaminants to treat, less energy needed to treat them. And we managed to do that not by talking about what we wanted but by talking about what the customer wanted. We were able to achieve our aims for the environment without constantly talking about the environment.

I think there's an important lesson there for anyone seeking change. If you can articulate your proposition so that it answers the needs of the target audience, you will have a much greater chance of succeeding.

I may not have felt nostalgic leaving BioTector that day, but afterwards, I found it very hard to go back and see people. I did it once and found it so difficult that I never went back. I was almost afraid I would start crying or something. Mom and Dad still owned the building, and kept their upstairs offices. They kept me posted with the news.

Now, five years on, I wouldn't change anything about my years in BioTector. I have great memories.

No Title

Not having a title anymore is quite odd. If somebody hands me a business card, I've nothing to give back to them. It took a while to be comfortable just being me. Because if you meet someone for the first time, the standard thing is to tell them who you are and what you do. It's difficult getting used to just being Dave.

At the moment, I'm involved in a range of projects, but my bumbling explanation can leave people confused or suspicious. About a year ago, I was bringing my father in law up for the first of a series of golf lessons. I said I'd hang around and hit a few balls in the next bay. We chatted with the instructor and he invited me into the lesson too. He zeroed in on one particular part of my game and said, "You'd really want to practise this – do you have time to do that at the minute?"

I said that I did, and of course then he asked me what I did. I was so evasive that he got the wrong end of the stick altogether.

When we finished up, I asked him what I owed him and he said, "Ah look, don't worry about it. Just come on up with Kevin the next time and you can take part in the lesson. No charge."

I had done such a lousy job of explaining myself that he thought I was out of work.

Get in Touch

So what do I do now?

Myself, Mom and Dad still work together. We find people who are extremely capable and who understand their industry really well and we invest in them. So far, we have five main investments, in Ireland and further afield. When we began in 2014, bank lending rates were very high, so we became a source of finance for great companies that would struggle to get the funds anywhere else.

One of the ones we invested in is the Von der Heyden Group. They're a fantastic company with a wonderful strategy and brilliant people. They ticked all of the BioTector boxes. So we came in with capital and got to accompany them on this wonderful journey they've been on over the last five years. We've learned a huge amount from them, and from the other companies we've invested in.

As these ventures start to close out over the coming years, one of my tasks will be to find new ones to take their place. The model is to find a partner that has the sectoral expertise that we can learn from and build upon. We don't want to invest in something we know nothing about – that's the easiest way to lose money. Instead we partner with people, learn about what they do and take the journey with them. We're there for advice and support on strategy, but they remain the industry experts.

I've often heard successful CEOs say that their company was an overnight success after twenty five years. It was the same with BioTector. We had been on the go for over twenty years before we finally sold. The overnight success bit comes right at the end, but you don't get there without going through all of the intermediate stages. There are rarely shortcuts; if you take them, you usually end up in the wrong place. Because we've been through it all before, we're well placed to identify the parts of the business you can accelerate, the parts you can't and the parts which are not yet fully understood. We can help determine how best to spend in order to ensure the best return. And so we offer an alternative to the venture capital model. We come in, we get to know you. If there's a fit, if we think we can help, we'll come on the journey with you.

We welcome contact from anyone who has a company which they think might be suited to our approach.

Acknowledgements

BioTector's success came as a result of so many fantastic, dedicated and capable people. In writing this book, it has been very important to me to acknowledge all those who made this such an amazing journey. I would like to thank all the BioTector team. I have never been able to put into words what a privilege it was to work alongside this wonderful group of people. I would also like to remember our financial controller, Margaret Fuentes, whose untimely passing shocked us all. She was an integral part of the BioTector story and such a kind and generous person.

Thank you to all of our distributors across the world who believed in our products and became an extension of our company. To our many loyal clients, thank you for giving us a chance, and supporting our growth through constructive feedback and a willingness to try our products in new applications. Thank you to Enterprise Ireland for their guidance, as well as their many educational and financial supports. Finally, I would like to thank John Hearne for helping me to write the BioTector story, and making the process so enjoyable.